Do-it-yourself

PROBATE

LAW PACK™
GUIDE

Probate Guide

First edition 1997
Second edition 2000

© 1997, 2000 Law Pack Publishing Limited

Law Pack Publishing Limited
10-16 Cole Street
London SE1 4YH

www.lawpack.co.uk

Printed in Great Britain

ISBN: 1 902646 27 4

Important facts

This **Law Pack** Guide contains the information, instruction and forms necessary to obtain a grant of probate or letters of administration, and administer an estate without a solicitor. This Guide is for use in England or Wales. It is not suitable for use in Scotland or Northern Ireland.

The information it contains has been carefully compiled from professional sources, but its accuracy is not guaranteed, as laws and regulations may change or be subject to differing interpretations.

Neither this nor any other publication can take the place of a solicitor on important legal matters. As with any legal matter, common sense should determine whether you need the assistance of a solicitor rather than rely solely on the information and forms in this **Law Pack** Guide.

We strongly urge you to consult a solicitor if:

- substantial amounts of money are involved;
- you do not understand the instructions or are uncertain how to complete and use a form correctly;
- what you want to do is not precisely covered by this Guide;
- trusts or business interests are involved.

Table of contents

How to use this Law Pack Guide vii

Introduction ix

Probate and the administration of an estate:
an overview xi

1   What is an executor? 1

2   When death occurs 7

3   Duties of an executor 13

4   Taking stock 19

5   Applying for a grant 29

6   Administering an estate 41

Glossary of useful terms 47

Appendices 51

Example forms in this guide 59

Index 95

How to use this Law Pack Guide

This **Law Pack** Guide can help you achieve an important legal objective conveniently, efficiently and economically. Remember that it is important for you to use this guide properly if you are to avoid later difficulties.

Step-by-step instructions for using this guide:

1. Read this guide carefully. If after thorough examination you decide that your requirements are not met by this **Law Pack** Guide, or you do not feel confident about writing your own documents, consult a solicitor.

2. At the end of this guide there are completed examples of probate forms for reference. Contact your local Probate Registry to obtain your copies of these forms. See page 52 for a full list.

3. Once obtained, make several copies of the original forms for practice, for future use and for updates. You should also make copies of the completed forms. Create a record-keeping system for both sets of copies.

4. When completing a form, do not leave any section blank, unless instructed otherwise. If any section is inapplicable, write 'not applicable', 'none' or 'nil' to show you have not overlooked the section.

5. Always use a pen or type on legal documents; never use pencil.

6. Do not cross out or erase anything you have written on your final forms.

7. You will find a helpful glossary of terms at the end of this **Law Pack** Guide. Refer to this glossary if you find unfamiliar terms.

8. Always keep legal documents in a safe place and in a location known to your spouse, family or solicitor.

Introduction

Ideally you are reading this **Law Pack** Probate Guide to prepare yourself for future eventualities. Perhaps you know you have been named executor in someone's Will. Or you are writing your own Will and want to know more about the duties of executors.

Most people would admit to knowing little about how probate – the procedure of taking out a 'grant of probate' and subsequent administration of an estate – works. One's first encounter with it is usually after the death of a loved one.

More often than not people are taken by surprise when told they have been named an executor – or 'executrix' if female – in a deceased's Will. The executor may have no knowledge of the deceased's wishes or the whereabouts, let alone the contents, of the Will and other important documents. The funeral and disposal of the testator's remains may have to be carried out without reference to their wishes simply because the Will has not been found. Sometimes those who have been named executors are unable to fulfil their duties and a beneficiary of the estate may need to act as administrator of the estate. When these complications, along with all the other responsibilities that must be attended to following a death, come to light during the mourning period, it becomes clear why it is best to be well prepared for the responsibilities of executorship.

This **Law Pack** Probate Guide is intended for those preparing for such responsibilities.

Probate and the administration of an estate: an overview

1. Register death and obtain copies of the death certificate.

2. Attend to the funeral, burial, cremation, etc.

3. Find and review the deceased's Last Will and Testament.

4. Determine who the executors are and whether they are able and willing to act. If not or if the deceased did not leave a valid Will, determine who will act as administrators of the estate. Get the agreement of the personal representatives in writing.

5. Apply to the Personal Application Department of the most accessible and convenient Probate Registry for the forms required.

6. Secure the house and/or other property of the deceased, insuring the house, car and any other valuable items as necessary.

7. Organise yourself for valuing assets, corresponding with others, keeping financial records and receiving the deceased's mail. Open an executors' bank account.

8. Write to all financial and business organisations in which the deceased had an interest. Include a copy of the death certificate and request the necessary information for the probate application.

9. List the deceased's assets and liabilities. Review them. Is it necessary to apply for a grant of probate? If the estate appears to be insolvent or there are other complexities, see a solicitor.

10. If the estate appears to be worth more than £234,000 make arrangements to raise money, e.g. by borrowing or by selling some of the deceased's personal property, to pay inheritance tax before the grant of probate can be issued.

11. Fill out probate forms as information is collected and return them to the Probate Registry.

12. When the Probate Registry contacts the executors, all executors visit the Registry or local office to sign or swear the necessary forms and pay probate fees.

13. Pay any inheritance tax due at the time of application and arrange for instalment payments if any of the assets qualify.

14. The Probate Registry sends the grant of probate to you by post along with any additional copies (sealed copies) ordered.

15. Send copies of the grant to each organisation contacted in Step 8 to show the executors' entitlement to deal with the deceased's assets. In return, organisations release the deceased's assets to the executors and close or transfer the deceased's accounts and files.

16. Advertise for creditors, if necessary. If any large or unexpected claims result, you should consider consulting a solicitor.

17. Respond to any queries raised by the Inland Revenue concerning the values of assets or liabilities of the estate. Agree final figures with them. Report any additional assets or liabilities that have come to light since probate was granted.

18. When all assets are collected, pay debts, including any unpaid income tax and capital gains tax relating to the deceased's income up to the time of death.

19. Ask the Inspector of Taxes for an income tax return and complete it with details of the income of the estate to the end of the tax year during which the deceased died. Pay any tax due. A return may also be needed for each subsequent tax year if the administration of the estate is not complete within one tax year.

20. Ask the Inland Revenue's Capital Taxes Office for *Form 30 (Application for formal discharge from inheritance tax)*; complete it and in due course receive the signed discharge certificate from the Revenue.

21. Check that there have been no claims against the estate under the Inheritance (Provision for Family and Dependants) Act 1975 during the six months following the grant of probate. Barring any such challenges to the Will, the estate can be distributed.

22. When all the assets have been accounted for and debts paid, legacies can be distributed. Get a receipt from each beneficiary.

23. When all cheques have cleared, close the executors' account.

24. Draw up estate accounts. Get approval of the accounts from all residuary beneficiaries and send them copies. Issue *Inland Revenue Form R185 (Estate Income)* to the residuary beneficiaries showing their shares of the income of the estate and the tax deducted from it during the tax year.

25. The administration of the estate is now complete. All accounts should be saved for 12 years.

What is an executor?

When someone is named the executor of a Will, he or she is being asked to take responsibility for administering the estate of the person who made the Will, called the *testator,* upon the testator's death. Acting as an executor should not be undertaken lightly. Immediately following the death the executors are expected to begin their administrative duties; long after other mourners' lives have returned to normal, the executors will still be administering the estate. This entails corresponding with other parties, keeping meticulous records, filling out forms and being answerable to creditors, beneficiaries and the intentions of the deceased, as recorded in the Will.

Do not be put off by the term 'estate'. This simply refers to all the property a person leaves behind, whether its value be hundreds or millions of pounds. One person's assets may include homes, yachts and a Swiss bank account, while another leaves a wedding ring, some changes of clothes and a shoe-box full of costume jewellery. Both have left estates to be accounted for and distributed.

Executors' duties can be summed up as: taking an inventory of the deceased's possessions and debts, collecting the assets, paying the bills and distributing the legacies (whether specific items, cash sums or residue) following the testator's wishes as closely as possible. This Guide takes you the probate process, without the services of a solicitor.

Grant of probate

Executors have the power to deal with the deceased's assets from the date of death, but not until they receive what is called a *grant of probate* can they prove their authority to those institutions and authorities that hold assets in the deceased's name. Grants of probate are issued by the High Court through Probate Registries.

More than one executor

If the Will appoints only one executor, or if only one person is able and willing to act, a grant of probate can be issued to one person. If the Will appoints more than four executors, only four of them will be allowed to take out the grant of probate. The others may renounce their right to apply for probate. Or they may decide not to apply for the time being but to reserve their right to apply in the future so that if, for example, one of the acting executors dies before the estate has been fully administered, the executor with power reserved may take his or her place.

If only one executor is taking out the grant of probate, it may be prudent for the other executor(s) to sign what's called a *power reserved letter*, even if it is not anticipated that he or she will want to apply at any stage. By reserving the right to apply in this way, a non-acting executor can step in if the acting executor becomes incapacitated before the administration of the estate is complete. The Probate Registry (see Appendix 1) provides a form necessary to renounce or reserve the right to apply for probate.

No matter how many executors are named, for practical purposes it is usually easier if one of the executors undertakes the administrative tasks on behalf of them all (he or she is referred to in this Guide as the *first applicant*). The executors should meet to discuss the practical side of carrying out their duties. Whatever is agreed should be put in writing and signed by them all. In fact, all official paperwork must be signed by all executors, even if they agree that one of them is the first applicant.

Caution: if it looks as though the deceased's estate is insolvent, i.e. the debts of the deceased and other liabilities of the estate, including funeral expenses, will exceed the value of the assets in the estate, executors should think carefully before applying for the grant of probate. If the estate may be insolvent, it is prudent to seek the advice of a solicitor before taking any further steps.

Other personal representatives

If an executor renounces the right to take out the grant of probate, any substitute executor named in the Will steps in and proceeds to apply for the grant of probate. If no executor is named in the Will or if the executor named cannot or does not wish to act and no substitute is named, beneficiaries can apply to act as the deceased's *personal representatives*. A beneficiary acting as the testator's personal representative is known as the *administrator*; the grant itself is called a *grant of letters of administration with Will annexed*. An administrator's duties are essentially the same as those of an executor. This Guide refers to executors, but the rights and responsibilities of both are the same in most respects, whether the person doing the work is an executor or an administrator.

Beneficiaries may apply for a grant as the deceased's administrators in the following order of priority:

    (1)   any residuary legatee;

    (2)   any personal representative of a residuary legatee;

    (3)   any other legatee;

    (4)   any personal representative of any other legatee;

    (5)   any creditor.

A minor (someone under the age of 18) may not act as an executor. If a minor is the only executor appointed in a Will, his or her parents or guardian are entitled to take out a grant of letters of administration with Will annexed on his behalf. The minor has the right to apply for the grant of probate on attaining his or her 18th birthday, if the administration of the estate has not been completed.

If the deceased left no Will, he or she is said to have died *intestate* and the estate is distributed in accordance with the rules of intestacy. The personal representatives are, again, known as administrators and the grant is called a *grant of letters of administration*. When there is no Will administrators are appointed in the following order of priority:

(1)   the deceased's spouse;

(2)   any child of the deceased and any issue of a child who died before the deceased;

(3)   the parents of the deceased;

(4)   brothers and sisters of the whole blood of the deceased and the issue of any who died before the deceased;

(5)   brothers and sisters of the half blood of the deceased and the issue of any who died before the deceased;

(6)   grandparents of the deceased;

(7)   uncles and aunts of the whole blood and the issue of any who died before the deceased;

(8)   uncles and aunts of the half blood and the issue of any who died before the deceased.

The maximum number of administrators is four, whether there is a Will or the person died intestate. A sole administrator may take out the grant only where none of the beneficiaries is under 18 or where no *life interest* arises. If either of these is the case, the grant must issue to a minimum of two administrators.

A life interest most commonly arises where the deceased's estate is worth more than £125,000 and he or she died intestate leaving a spouse and a child or children. In that case, the spouse will take the first £125,000 as a legacy, all the personal chattels, and will have a life interest in half of the residue of the estate. The remaining half of the estate is held in trust for the child or children until reaching 18; they also benefit from the spouse's life interest or his/her death.

Highlight

A sole administrator may take out the grant only where none of the beneficiaries is under 18 or where no life interest arises.

Should a solicitor be instructed? ▬▬

Executors can instruct a solicitor, stockbroker or other advisor to perform specific duties even if they do not use a solicitor to make the probate application. Whether an executor handles all the tasks involved in administering the estate or uses professional advisors is a matter of choice and convenience. Any fees properly incurred are paid out of the estate.

This Law Pack Guide is designed to help the lay person sort out a simple, straightforward Will or intestacy. If the Will or the estate is complex, a solicitor should be consulted. If you are in any doubt, seek professional advice. Some signs that a solicitor should be involved include the following:

(1)   the estate is insolvent;

(2)   a beneficiary cannot be contacted;

(3)   someone intends to challenge the Will;

(4)   there is some question of the Will's validity, or the Will cannot be found;

(5)   someone stands to inherit a life interest in the estate;

(6)   beneficiaries include children under the age of 18 and a trust is set up for them;

(7)   the deceased owned a business or was a partner in a business;

(8)   the deceased was a Name, i.e. investor, in Lloyds of London insurance market;

(9)   a trust is set up under the Will;

(10) any house or land in the estate has an unregistered title.

When death occurs 2

When someone dies a doctor should be called. He or she will issue a medical certificate stating the cause or causes of death, along with a notice setting out who is eligible to register the death with the local Registrar of Births and Deaths.

Registering the death

If the death has occurred inside a house or public building, the following people may act as informant, in the following order:

(1)   a relative of the deceased who was present at the death;

(2)   a relative of the deceased who was present during the final stages of the illness;

(3)   a relative of the deceased who lives in the district where the death occurred;

(4)   anyone who was present at the death;

(5)   someone in authority in the building where the death occurred who was aware of the circumstances of the death, e.g. the owner of a nursing home or the warden of sheltered accommodation;

(6)   any resident of the building where the death occurred, if he or she was aware of the circumstances of the death;

(7)   the person who accepts responsibility for arranging the funeral.

If the death occurred outside a house or public building, the following people are eligible to register the death in the following order:

(1)   a relative of the deceased able to provide the Registrar with the necessary details;

(2)   anyone who was present at the death;

(3)   the person who found the body;

(4)   the person in charge of the body (the police if the body is unidentified);

(5)   the person who accepts responsibility for arranging the funeral.

Within five days of the death, the informant must take the medical certificate to the Registrar of Deaths, or must send written notice. The deceased's medical card should be given to the Registrar as well. The Registrar will ask for other details about the deceased:

(1)   the date and place of death;

(2)   the full name of the deceased, including any maiden name;

(3)   the date and place of birth of the deceased.;

(4)   the occupation of the deceased;

(5)   the name, date of birth and occupation of the deceased's spouse, whether or not still living;

(6)   the deceased's usual address;

(7)   whether the deceased received any state pension or allowance;

(8)   the date of birth of any surviving spouse.

The death certificate

Once the death has been registered, the informant will be given a death certificate, which is a copy of the entry on the register. There is a small charge for each copy, and it is sensible to get three or four copies. The executors will need to send copies to

Highlight

Within five days of the death, the informant must take the medical certificate to the Registrar of Deaths, or must send written notice.

the deceased's bank, to the registrars of companies in which he or she held shares, to insurance companies holding policies written in trust and to the Probate Registry. Although you can have the certificate returned to you once it has been inspected, it is more convenient to circulate several copies at once.

Note: A while after the death the cost of a copy of the death certificate may increase. The period varies depending on the register office so it is worth checking if it is probable further copies will be needed.

The Will

If the executors are prepared for their duties, they may have been in possession of a copy of the Will even before the death and know the location of the original. They may know of the deceased's instructions concerning organ donation, disposal of the body and funeral wishes. All of this information is needed in the first hours following death.

Arranging the funeral is not specifically the duty of executors and should be handled by whoever is most aware of the deceased's wishes. But anyone who manages the funeral is entitled to have the account settled out of money from the estate.

If there is no opportunity for preparation before the death the Will must be located to determine who has been named its executor(s). If no Will is found at the deceased's home, it may have been sent to his or her bank or solicitor for safekeeping. It may have been deposited at Somerset House, in which case a deposit certificate will have been issued on receipt of the Will; the Will can be reclaimed by sending the certificate to:

> The Principal Registry
> Family Division
> Safe Custody Department
> First Avenue House
> 42–49 High Holborn
> London WC1V 2NP

If a Will is found, ascertain that it is the deceased's last Will by making enquiries at the deceased's bank and solicitor, for example. It must bear the signature of the deceased and of two witnesses. Probate may be granted on a copy, but you should notify the Probate Registry as soon as possible that the original cannot be found. The Registry will tell you what evidence is needed as proof that the original Will had not been revoked by being destroyed before death.

The necessity of a formal 'reading of the Will' before hopeful beneficiaries, or a solicitor, is a myth. There is no legal requirement for any such reading but it is courteous to write to beneficiaries to inform them of their entitlement under the Will.

There may be some doubt as to who the beneficiaries are under the Will. Many Wills describe certain beneficiaries in terms of groups of people, for example 'my children,' rather than naming them. The expression 'my children' includes, by law, children conceived at the time of the deceased's death and subsequently born alive, adopted children and legitimated children (children born to unmarried parents who later marry).

If the Will was executed after 3 April 1988, children whose parents were married to each other at the time of their birth are treated in the same way as those whose parents were not, even if the executors have no knowledge of the children's existence. If the Will was executed before then, the executors will not be liable to a testator's child born outside marriage if they did not know of his or her existence. These rules apply unless it is clear from the Will that the deceased intended otherwise.

Generally, if a beneficiary named in a Will has died before the testator, the gift to him or her will simply not take effect. However, if that beneficiary is a child, grand-child or great-grandchild of the testator, and he or she has left children of his or her own, the children step into their parent's shoes and their entitlement under the Will, shared equally between them.

If the deceased married after making the Will and the Will was not expressed to be in expectation of the marriage, the Will is automatically revoked. Divorce, however, does not revoke a Will, but the former spouse is treated as if he or she died on the date of the divorce so that he or she cannot take a gift under the Will or act as an executor.

Highlight

There is no legal requirement for a formal 'reading of the Will'.

Highlight

If a beneficiary (who is a child of the testator) has died before the testator, his or her children share the entitlement.

If the executors are uncertain as to the interpretation of other parts of the Will, they should seek the advice of a solicitor to avoid the risk of distributing the money wrongly.

Once probate is granted the Will becomes a public document, but until then the beneficiaries may know nothing of their legacies, unless the deceased told them before he or she died. However, the executors will usually tell the beneficiaries that they have been left a legacy although it is impossible to be specific about the amount if it is a legacy of residue or part of residue. But no legacy can be guaranteed at this stage as the Will may be found invalid, may be challenged, or the assets of the estate may not be sufficient to pay all the legacies.

Duties of executors 3

In preparation for dealing with the assets and liabilities of the estate, some administrative tasks should be attended to by the executors as soon as possible.

Have the deceased's postal address changed to that of the first applicant, the executor who is to handle day-to-day business and personal affairs. If the home is to be left unoccupied the executors should ensure that it is securely locked; that water, electricity and gas supplies have been turned off and mail re-directed.

The executors should also ensure that there are both current buildings and contents insurance policies on the home. The executors may be held liable by any beneficiary who receives less from the estate than he or she should because of a burglary, fire or other loss. The insurers should be notified of the death and given the names and addresses of the executors. If there are particularly valuable items at the deceased's home and it is to be left unoccupied, it may be better to remove them for safekeeping.

Finally, the executors should open an executors' bank account into which they will eventually deposit the proceeds of assets and from which they will pay the bills of the deceased.

Make a thorough search of the deceased's papers for the documents that will be needed to finalise the deceased's affairs. These will include:

- cheque books;
- bank statements;

- savings certificates and other national savings assets;

- outstanding bills;

- share certificates and stockbroker's details;

- car registration documents;

- mortgage papers;

- insurance and pension documentation;

- information on jewellery and collectibles, e.g. insurance valuations;

- tax assessments, returns and other tax papers.

The executor's aims are to:

(1) identify the assets of the estate and assess their approximate value;

(2) identify the deceased's debts and pay them;

(3) distribute the legacies.

Is a grant of probate necessary? —

While itemising the assets of the estate, the executors must bear in mind that it may not be necessary to apply for a grant of probate. Whether or not a grant is required depends not only on the size of the deceased's estate, but also on the kinds of assets in it.

For example, if the deceased only left a great deal of cash, personal items having a high market value and a very expensive car, there is no need to apply for a grant of probate because executors need no formal proof of their authority to distribute such assets. On the other hand, if the deceased had a bank account and shares, or if the deceased's home needs to be sold or transferred to a beneficiary, a grant will be necessary so the executors can show they are entitled to deal with these assets.

Certain authorities can pay sums due on death to the person entitled under a Will or intestacy without requiring sight of a grant of probate, as long as the amount payable is less than £5,000 per asset. The assets concerned include:

Highlight

Whether or not a grant is required depends not only on the size of the deceased's estate, but also on the kinds of assets in it.

- **National Savings, including prizes won on Premium Bonds.** In order to claim, the executors need to complete *Form NSA 904*, which is available from post offices, and send it to the address given on that form for the type of account held, together with a registrar's copy of the death certificate.

- **Building society accounts, deposits with friendly societies, trade union deposits of members, arrears of salary or pension due to government or local government employees and police and firemens pensions.** The executors should write to the relevant authority, asking for a claim form and sending a registrar's copy of the death certificate.

Other assets that may be realised without the executors needing to produce the grant of probate are:

- **Nominated property.** Until 1981, the holder of certain National Savings investments and government stock could nominate someone to receive them on his death. After 1981, no new nominations could be made, but those made before that year are valid. Such a nomination takes effect independently of the deceased's Will or intestacy and independently of any grant of probate. The person nominated can have such stocks transferred into his or her name or redeemed on producing the death certificate. There is no upper limit on the value of the nominated property which can be dealt with in this way, but if the institution is concerned that the estate may be large enough for inheritance tax to be paid on it, it may require the executors to obtain a certificate from the Inland Revenue to show that any such tax has been paid.

- **Jointly held assets.** When two people hold property as joint tenants, on the death of one of them, his or her share of the asset passes directly to the other by right of survivorship, regardless of the provisions of the Will or the intestacy rules. Such assets might include a house or flat, or bank or building society accounts. No grant of probate is required to transfer the deceased's share of these assets to the surviving joint tenant. If the property is a house or flat, and the land is registered land, a registrar's copy of the death certificate should be sent to the Land Registry to enable the survivor to be registered as the sole surviving owner of the house or flat. If the land is unregistered land, a registrar's copy of the death certificate should be kept with the title deeds and will need to be produced when the land is sold. If the joint asset is a bank or building society account, a registrar's copy of the death certificate should be sent to the relevant bank or building society so the deceased's name may be removed from the account.

Therefore, if the deceased's estate consists solely of jointly held assets, there is no need for the executors to apply for a grant of probate.

Probate forms

The Probate Registry will supply the executors with the required forms, but it is best to ask for them early on in the probate process. As the inventory and valuation process progresses, executors can fill in the forms as they go along. Probate forms are discussed in more detail in chapter 5.

A note on Probate Registries: all executors will need to make at least one visit to the Probate Registry or a local office. Apart from the Principal Registry in London, there are district Registries and local offices under their control throughout the country (see Appendix 1 pages 52–56). It is sensible to choose a Registry or local office conveniently located for the executors; bear in mind that some local offices do have minimal and sporadic office hours which may not necessarily result in a quick or convenient service, and that not all Probate Registries have identical procedures.

Financial records

During the administration of the estate, the executors must keep track of every financial transaction, no matter how small. The money and assets belonging to the estate must be kept entirely separate from the executors' personal money and assets. Out-of-pocket expenses of the executors should be recorded as carefully as the payment of bank and probate fees or inheritance taxes.

Although executors are paid for their efforts only if the Will so specifies, expenses the executors incur such as postage, travel costs, telephone bills, etc., can be paid from the estate.

More importantly, the executors must be able to account for every penny of the testator's estate. They have a fiduciary responsibility (i.e. one of trust) to the creditors and beneficiaries of the estate. When the estate has been fully administered, the executors will need to draw up accounts to demonstrate to the beneficiaries how the assets of the estate were spent or distributed. Spotless, unimpeachable financial records are the executors' proof of what has occurred within the testator's estate, from the date of death to the date of the final distribution of assets.

Paying inheritance tax

Probate poses a conundrum: once a thorough valuation of the deceased's assets and liabilities is completed, any inheritance tax due must be paid *before* applying for the grant of probate. However, few financial institutions will hand over the funds of the deceased until there is a grant of probate to prove the executors' authority.

If the deceased had funds in a National Savings account or held National Savings Certificates and Premium Bonds, National Savings may issue a cheque in favour of the Inland Revenue and send it directly to the Probate Registry to cover all or part of the tax, thereby permitting the Registry to issue the grant of probate. Similar arrangements may be made between a building society account and the Inland Revenue. Other banks may be willing to arrange a loan to the executors to pay the inheritance tax, thereby releasing the funds to repay the loan. Further details are provided in chapter 4.

Identifying beneficiaries

Once the liabilities of the estate have been paid, the executors identify the beneficiaries of the estate: either those named in the Will or those entitled under the intestacy rules. If the executors distribute the estate incorrectly, they are personally liable to the rightful beneficiaries and to creditors about whom they know or should have known.

To protect themselves from unknown creditors and beneficiaries, the executors can follow a statutory procedure which involves the placing of advertisements for creditors in the *London Gazette* at:

> The London Gazette
> PO Box 7923
> London SE1 5ZH
> Tel 020 7394 4580

They must also advertise in a newspaper circulating in the area where the deceased lived and, particularly if he or she owned a business, the area where he or she worked at the time of death. If land is to be distributed, an advertisement should also be placed in a newspaper circulating in the district where the land is situated.

The advertisements should state that anyone with a claim against or an interest in the estate must make their claim known within a stated time (not less than two months) from the date of the notice, after which the executors may distribute the estate, having regard only to those claims of which they have notice. After the stated time, anyone who has not come forward cannot make a claim against the executors, although they may claim against the beneficiaries of the estate into whose hands assets have passed.

Advertising for unknown creditors may not be necessary if there is no reason to suspect that the deceased has incurred debts other than those known to the executor.

Note: unlike an executor, an administrator can place statutory advertisements only after the grant of letters of administration has been issued.

Taking stock

4

As a first step, the executors should list those assets which they know, based on personal observation or findings, the deceased owned. This chapter includes a checklist beginning on page 20 which sets out the most commonly owned assets.

Following this inventory by observation, the executor sends notification of the death to the deceased's bank, building society, accountant, insurance company and other institutions. The letters to the bank and building society should request information about each account and instruct them to stop all unpaid cheques and standing orders. Also ask for a list of deeds and other documents held on behalf of the deceased, e.g. life policies, as at the date of death. Executors do not have to wait to receive the grant of probate to begin this notification and inventory, but a copy must be sent to each institution when it is received from the Probate Registry. For the initial correspondence, it is sufficient to enclose a copy of the death certificate.

The goal is to get in writing the value of all the assets and debts as at the time of death. This information must be provided on the probate forms. Even if an asset is left as a legacy to a beneficiary, it must be listed and accounted for in the inventory.

Valuing debts

The following is a checklist of debts the deceased might owe. Information on any of these liabilities that apply should be included in section F of probate *Form IHT200*. This is the return of the testator's whole estate for inheritance tax purposes (see page 64 for completed example). If necessary, it is generally possible to request a delay in payment of debts until the grant has been obtained and funds are available.

(1)   water rates
(2)   telephone bill
} ask for a bill to the date of death;

(3)   electricity bill
(4)   gas bill
} take a meter reading on the date of death, or as soon afterwards as possible and ask for a bill to that date;

(5)   loan or overdraft } write to the bank for the outstanding balance;

(6)   credit card bills } write to the credit card company asking for the amount of any outstanding balance;

(7)   mail-order catalogue bill } write to notify the company on the death and to ask whether any outstanding balance is due;

(8)   rent arrears;

(9)   hire purchase payments;

(10) debts owed by the deceased to other individuals;

(11) outstanding income tax and capital gains tax.

Reasonable funeral expenses are also counted as a liability of the estate, including the cost of a grave-stone; these should be included in section F of *Form IHT200*. If the person arranging the funeral is in receipt of Income Support, Working Family Tax Credit or Housing Benefit, he or she can apply to the Social Fund (a loan-type scheme administered by the Benefits Agency) for a payment to cover reasonable funeral expenses. However, the cost is repaid out of the estate if money subsequently becomes available.

Asset checklist

To help the executors make an inventory of assets, the following checklist itemises some of the typical ones found in an estate. As you go through it, refer to the completed examples of forms (beginning on page 60) which must be filed with the Probate

Highlight

Generally, the value reported for probate purposes should be the price an asset would fetch if sold on the open market on the date of death.

Registry. Not all the assets listed here are specifically categorised on *Form IHT200*; those not listed should be recorded on *Supplementary page D17* and their total value included in F23 of *Form IHT200* (see page 64 for completed example). Generally, the value reported for probate purposes should be the price an asset would fetch if sold on the open market on the date of death.

House or flat

If the deceased owned his or her own home jointly with another person, only the deceased's share of the home is treated as part of his or her estate. It will usually be a half-share unless the owners held the property as beneficial tenants in common and the title deeds specify that they hold it in unequal shares. If two or more joint owners hold a property as beneficial tenants in common, each person can leave his or her own share of the property to whoever he or she wishes under his or her Will. However, if they hold the property as beneficial joint tenants, the share of a person who dies automatically passes to the survivor or survivors.

If the precise value is not relevant for calculating the inheritance tax due on the estate, for example because the property or the deceased's share of it is to go to the deceased's spouse, an approximate value will normally be acceptable (see page 36). The executor may estimate the value himself, by reference to the prices which similar properties in the area are fetching, or ask an estate agent for an informal valuation.

Highlight

An approximate house or flat value is usually acceptable if the property passes to the deceased's spouse

In some circumstances, it is better to ask an estate agent to make a formal valuation, for which a fee will be charged. For instance, if the property is to be transferred to a beneficiary as part of a legacy, instead of cash, it is normally best to have a formal valuation to ensure that the distribution among the beneficiaries is fair.

Whichever method is used, the value given will be checked by the District Valuer for the Inland Revenue, who may challenge it if it appears to be too low. If the property is sold soon after the death (although the executors will not be able to complete the sale until they have the grant showing their entitlement to deal with the property), the District Valuer may seek to substitute the sale price for the value submitted in the probate application. Details of the property should be included on *Supplementary page D12, Land, Buildings and Interest in Land* (see completed example on page 84).

If there is a mortgage on the deceased's house or flat, the mortgage lender should be notified. You should give the deceased's name, address and mortgage account number and enclose a copy of the death certificate. An example letter to a deceased's mortgage lender is provided on page 57. You will need to know how much of the mortgage was outstanding at the date of death, and whether there is a life assurance or mortgage protection policy linked to the mortgage. If there is, you should ask whether the cover is sufficient to repay the mortgage and whether there will be any surplus remaining after repayment.

Bank account

The executors must write to the deceased's bank and, if there is also a building society account, to the building society, with a registrar's copy of the death certificate, to inform them of the death and to instruct them to stop all unpaid cheques and standing orders. You should also ask for a list of all deeds, share certificates and other documents held on the deceased's behalf and the balances on the deceased's accounts at the date of death, with a separate figure for interest which had been earned on the money to that date, but not credited to the account. This information is needed for *Form IHT200*. It is also useful to ask, in the same letter, what interest has been credited to the deceased's account during the tax year in which he or she died and whether it was paid net of tax or gross. This information will be needed for the tax return to the date of death. An example of a letter to a deceased's bank is provided on page 58.

The executors will also need to open a bank account in their own names to enable them to pay in cheques for the proceeds of sales of assets of the estate, and to write cheques to discharge liabilities. The executors' full names and addresses should be given to the bank, which will send a mandate for completion and signature by the executors.

Any cheques which are made payable to the deceased but which were not paid into his or her account before the death can be paid

Highlight

Cheques which are made payable to the deceased but which were not paid into his or her account before the death can be paid into his or her account or the executors' account.

into his or her account or the executors' account. Once a copy of the grant of probate has been shown to the bank, the bank can transfer the balance on the deceased's account to the executors' account.

Stocks and shares

If the deceased owned any shares, the certificates may be at the deceased's home or with his or her bank, solicitor or stockbroker. If they are at the home and it is to be left unoccupied, it is best to remove them for safe-keeping. Check with the registrar of each of the companies in which the shares were held to make sure that the holdings evidenced by the certificates are correct. The name and address of the registrar can usually be found on the counterfoil of the share certificate or you can look them up in the *Register of Registrars*, a publication which can be found in most reference libraries.

Sometimes, shareholdings are in the nominee name of the shareholder's stockbroker and the stockbroker will have the share certificates. If that is the case, there is no need to write to each of the company registrars, but the stockbroker should be notified of the death and sent a copy of the death certificate.

If any share certificates cannot be found, the executors will need to sign a statutory declaration and indemnity before selling them or transferring them to a beneficiary, for which the registrar of the company will charge a fee. It states that the executors have searched for the certificate and believe it to be lost, and the executors indemnify the company against any loss if the certificate comes to light later in the hands of a person who has a better claim to ownership of the shares than the executors do.

Once a complete list of shareholdings has been compiled, the executors can ask a stockbroker for a probate valuation, for which he will charge a fee, generally a fixed sum per holding. Alternatively, executors may make their own valuation by referring to the *Stock Exchange Daily Official List* for the day the deceased died. The *List* is available at public libraries or it can be bought from the Publications Section of the Stock Exchange in London.

For probate purposes the value of a stock is the lower of the two values quoted, plus a quarter of the difference between those values, e.g. for a share quoted at 96–98p for that day, 96.5p would be the probate value.

If any of the shares are quoted 'XD' there is a dividend due to the deceased that has not yet been paid. If you are obtaining a valuation from a broker, he or she will include such dividends in the valuation. Otherwise, telephone the registrar of the company who will be able to give the value of the dividend. The dividend per share will be a gross figure. Multiply it by the number of shares held by the deceased and deduct tax at 10 per cent to arrive at the net figure which will appear on the dividend cheque.

The value of unit trust units can be obtained from the fund manager of the relevant unit trust company. If the deceased owned shares in any unquoted companies, write to the company secretary of each one asking for a valuation of the shares at the date of death.

A list of all shares and their values should be included on *Supplementary page D7* (see completed example on pages 79–80). Dividends (the net figure) should be listed separately as shown. Any dividends which were uncashed at the time of death should also be included. The total values are then included in Section F of *Form IHT200* (see completed example, page 64). If the deceased had a personal equity plan (PEP) or an Individual Savings Account (ISA) its provider can give a valuation as at the date of death.

Businesses

If the deceased had an interest in a business it will need to be valued by the business' accountant, backed up by a copy of the latest accounts, as requested in *Supplementary page D14* of *Form IHT200*.

Car

A local garage can provide an accurate valuation of the deceased's car. On the other hand, the executors may prefer simply to sell the car soon after the death and use the sale price as the value at the date of death.

Highlight

For probate purposes the value of a stock is the lower of the two values quoted, plus a quarter of the difference between those values.

Highlight

If the deceased had an interest in a business it will need to be valued by the business' accountant, backed up by a copy of the latest accounts.

Jewellery

An overall valuation will usually be acceptable for jewellery, although if an individual piece is worth more than £500 it should be valued separately. A jeweller can give a valuation, for which he or she will usually charge a fee. You should tell the jeweller that the valuation is needed for probate purposes to ensure you receive an estimate of the price for which he or she could sell the item, not the replacement value, which would be much higher.

Works of art

One way of finding out whether a particular painting or sculpture is of value is to see if it is separately listed on the deceased's home contents insurance policy. An art dealer can give a valuation of any works of art. Make it clear you are asking for the price it would fetch at auction at the date of death, not the value for which it should be insured.

Other possessions

There is no need to compile a detailed list of all of the deceased's possessions, including furniture and personal effects. An estimate of their total value can be given, based on what they might fetch if sold second-hand or, if appropriate, at auction at the date of death, although details of individual items worth over £500 should be given. The Inland Revenue can challenge asset values if they appear suspiciously low. In the case of a husband and wife, household possessions are generally treated as being held jointly between them, and so their total value should be divided by two to give the value of the deceased's share. Of course, if the deceased owned something outright, the entire value of the item is considered part of the deceased's estate for tax purposes.

National Savings

There is a special procedure for National Savings accounts. The executor must complete *Form NSA 904* (available at post offices) and send it to the address given on the form for that type of account. For National Savings certificates, the executor will need to write to National Savings asking for a letter confirming the value of the certificates held by the deceased at the date of death. The Probate Registry will need to see this letter.

Premium Bonds

You must notify the Bonds and Stock Office, Government Building, Lytham St. Anne's, Lancashire FY0 1YN, of the holder's death. Bonds can either be encashed or they can remain in the prize draw for 12 months after the death. If any prize is won, it can be claimed in the usual way by returning the winning bond to the Bonds and Stock Office, and the prize will belong to the estate to be distributed under the deceased's Will, or the intestacy if there is no Will. As long as the value of the bonds and any prize money does not exceed £5,000, there is no need to provide a copy of the grant of probate to receive payment. Premium Bonds are valued at their face value. They should also be listed on the National Savings *Form NSA 904*.

Outstanding salary or pension payments

If the deceased was employed at the time of death, a letter must be sent to his or her employer notifying them of the death and asking whether any salary or other payments are outstanding. However, the employer may need to see a copy of the grant of probate before paying those wages to the executors.

If the deceased belonged to a union or trade association, there may be a death benefit payable to his or her family. Likewise, if the deceased was receiving a pension, the scheme administrator or pension provider must be notified of the death and outstanding pension payments claimed.

Outstanding salary or pension payments should be included in *Form IHT200* as an asset of the estate. If the deceased was a member of an occupational pension scheme, a lump sum death benefit may be payable and you should write to the scheme administrator or pension provider to find out if that is the case.

Some benefits payable by an employer may be discretionary and not form part of the deceased's estate on death. This means that they do not pass under the deceased's Will or the intestacy and will not be subject to IHT or duty. These benefits would not need to be included in the *Form IHT200*.

Highlight

If the deceased belonged to a union or trade association, there may be a death benefit payable to his or her family.

Life assurance and pension policies

Write to the life assurance company or pension provider to notify them of the date of death, stating the policy number and enclosing a copy of a registrar's copy of the death certificate. Ask what sum is payable on the death and whether was it written in trust for any named person. If it was, the proceeds may be paid direct to that person on production of the death certificate. If not, the proceeds, including any bonuses, will generally be included as part of the deceased's estate and must be included in *Form IHT200*. Sometimes, the policy will be linked to a loan or mortgage, in which case the proceeds will be paid directly to the creditor, any excess being paid to the estate.

Taxes and bills

If the deceased paid income tax under PAYE (Pay As You Earn system) and/or received interest net of tax on bank or building society accounts, there may be a tax refund to claim. On the other hand, if income has been paid gross, or the deceased was a higher rate taxpayer, there may be additional income tax to pay. If the deceased sold any shares for example, there may also be capital gains tax to pay. In any event, the deceased's tax inspector must be informed of the death. He or she will send a tax return to be completed by the executors, relating to the period up to the time of death. Any tax refund is an asset of the estate (and any additional tax due is a liability of the estate) and must be included in *Form IHT200*.

Highlight

Any tax refund is an asset of the estate and must be included in Form IHT200.

A refund of Council Tax may be due. The deceased's home will be exempt from Council Tax if it is left empty from the date of death until probate has been granted, and for a further six months from the date of the grant. If the death leaves just one other person living in the property, the 25 per cent discount for single occupation may be claimed from the date of death. Any refund of Council Tax in respect of a period before the date of death must be included in *Form IHT200* as an asset of the estate.

Social Security payments

If the deceased was receiving a state retirement pension, the local DSS office should be notified of the death. The pension book should be sent with your letter inquiring whether there are any pension payments uncollected by the deceased. Any under-paid pension will be a debt due to the deceased and must be included in *Form IHT200* as an asset of the estate. If the deceased was receiving any other state benefits, these will also need to be stopped and any outstanding payments due up to the date of death claimed.

Foreign property

The value in sterling of property owned by the deceased outside the UK or debts owed to him or her by any resident outside the UK must be reported to the Probate Registry in *Supplementary page D15* of *Form IHT200*.

Applying for a grant

5

The forms

The forms necessary to apply for a grant of probate are available free of charge from the Personal Applications Department of the Principal Probate Registry in London or from the District Probate Registries (see the Appendix for details) and from the Inland Revenue's Capital Taxes Office (CTO, tel: 0845 234 1020).

Depending of the estate of the deceased, the forms to be completed are as below. Completed examples are provided in this Guide for guidance when filling in your own. These are based on two fictional estates that exemplify which forms are completed depending on the estate: Edward John Scott's and Michael Stephen Brown's.

1.   *Form PA1* asks for basic information about the deceased and for the names and addresses of the executors.

2.   *Form IHT200* or *Form IHT205* enable the Probate Registry to determine the probate fee and the CTO any inheritance tax and interest.

3.   **Supplementary pages** to be completed with *IHT200* to give the Inland Revenue further details of the deceased's assets.

Probate Registries issue *Forms PA1* and *IHT205,* while the CTO issues *Form IHT200* and its supplementary pages. (You will also receive *Forms* **PA2**, **IHT213** and **IHT206**; these contain guidance on completing *PA1, IHT200* and *IHT205,* respectively.)

Note: probate forms must be sent by post to a Controlling Probate Registry (see Appendix); they should not be sent to a local office, even if you want to be interviewed at a local office.

Before looking at the forms in detail, familiarise yourself with the steps and forms involved in obtaining a grant of probate by going through the following flowcharts.

Before probate appointment

Highlight

Probate forms must be sent to a Controlling Probate Registry; they should not be sent to the a local office, even if you wish to be interviewed at a local office.

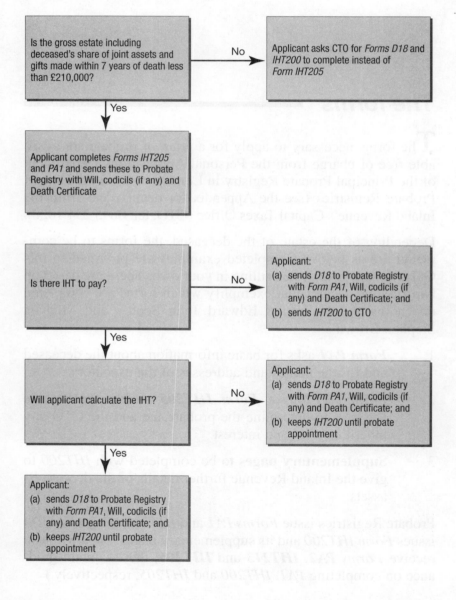

Is the gross estate including deceased's share of joint assets and gifts made within 7 years of death less than £210,000?

No → Applicant asks CTO for *Forms D18* and *IHT200* to complete instead of *Form IHT205*

Yes ↓

Applicant completes *Forms IHT205* and *PA1* and sends these to Probate Registry with Will, codicils (if any) and Death Certificate

Is there IHT to pay?

No → Applicant:
(a) sends *D18* to Probate Registry with *Form PA1*, Will, codicils (if any) and Death Certificate; and
(b) sends *IHT200* to CTO

Yes ↓

Will applicant calculate the IHT?

No → Applicant:
(a) sends *D18* to Probate Registry with *Form PA1*, Will, codicils (if any) and Death Certificate; and
(b) keeps *IHT200* until probate appointment

Yes ↓

Applicant:
(a) sends *D18* to Probate Registry with *Form PA1*, Will, codicils (if any) and Death Certificate; and
(b) keeps *IHT200* until probate appointment

After probate appointment

The probate fee is paid at the probate appointment. If the applicant has completed a *Form IHT205*, the Probate Registry will issue the grant by post after the appointment and without any further formalities. However, where the application requires a *Form IHT200*, there are further formalities as set out below before the Probate Registry can issue the grant.

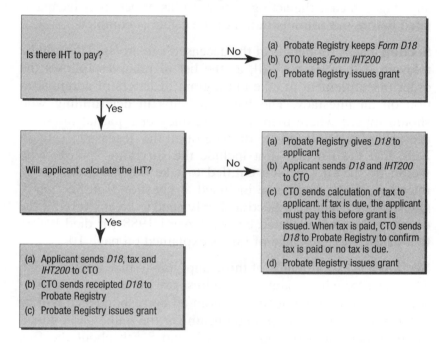

Form PA1—Probate Application Form (see page 60 for completed example, Edward John Scott's estate)

Section 1 asks which Probate Registry or local office you wish to be interviewed at.

Section 2 asks for the deceased's full name, address, occupation, dates of birth and death, age and marital status and details of any assets of the estate which are held in a name other than the deceased's.

Section 3 asks whether there is a Will and whether a gift is made under it to a person under 18. If so, the executors (or the trustees if the Will appoints trustees) will hold the minor beneficiary's gift until the beneficiary is 18. Question 4 asks for the names of any executors and, if any of the named executors are not applying for probate, why that is the case. If a named executor gives reason D ('does not wish to apply now but may later'), the Probate Registry will provide a power reserved letter for him or her to sign. Where only one executor is taking out the grant it may be prudent for a non-acting executor to sign a power reserved letter, even if it is not anticipated that he or she will want to apply at any stage, in case the acting executor dies or becomes incapacitated before the administration of the estate is complete.

Section 4 asks for details of the deceased's relatives. This will be relevant if there is no Will, as the list of relatives follows the order of entitlement to take out a grant of letters of administration on an intestacy. The list also helps in determining who should inherit where there is an intestacy or a partial intestacy (i.e. where the Will fails to dispose of all the deceased's estate). Note that the list does not include the surviving spouse, who would be the first person entitled to take out the grant on an intestacy; those details are included at question 9 in Section 5. Questions 4, 5 and 6 of Section 4 only need to be answered if the deceased left a Will dated before 4 April 1988 (or died before that date). The relevance of this is explained on page 10.

Section 5 asks for details of those applying to take out the grant. The executor whose name and address are given at questions 1-4 will be the first applicant to whom all correspondence will be addressed. There is space underneath for the name and address of the other executors. Questions 7 and 8 ask about the first applicant's relationship to the deceased. This information is needed for the oath which will be sworn at the Probate Registry on application for the grant. More importantly, in the case of an intestacy, this information verifies that the applicant is the person entitled to take out the grant of letters of administration.

Form IHT205 Short Form for Personal Applicants (see page 86 for completed example, Michael Stephen Brown's estate)

If you can answer 'no' to all the Preliminary Questions on page 2 of this form there is no need to complete *Form IHT200*; continue to answer the questions on pages 3 and 4. If any of the answers to the preliminary questions is 'yes', *IHT200* must be completed, in which case you should answer only the questions on page 2 of *Form IHT205* and send it to the Probate Registry with *Form IHT200. Form IHT206* contains notes to help you with *Form IHT205.*

Form IHT200 Full Account for Personal Applicants
(see page 64 for completed example, Edward John Scott's estate)

The questions on this form are similar to those on *Form IHT205* but they require fuller details. There may be a number of supplementary pages to complete with the *Form IHT200* as in our example. If there is insufficient space for all the information asked for, you should attach a separate sheet of paper and include the total on *Form IHT200* itself. *Form IHT213* will help you answer the questions. If the estate includes land or buildings *Supplementary page D12* should also be completed. If it includes stocks and shares, list the details on *Supplementary page D7. Supplementary pages D4, D3, D5* and *D6* deal with nominated property, gifts, assets held in trust and death benefits payable under pension policies. These may not appear to be part of the estate, but they may need to be taken into account in order to calculate inheritance tax. *Supplementary page D4* also deals with jointly-held property and land and buildings (whether inside the UK or not).

The inheritance tax on some types of property may be paid by instalments (see page 36) and page 5 of the form includes a box to be ticked, should you wish to do that.

In sections H and J on pages 6 and 7 of *IHT200* the executors have the choice of either calculating any inheritance tax themselves or leaving it to the CTO to work out (by leaving these sections blank).

All the executors should read the Declaration on page 8 of *Form IHT200* and sign it.

Supplementary page D7 Stocks and Shares
(see page 79 for completed example, Edward John Scott's estate)

If the deceased owned stocks or shares, the details of those holdings should be entered on this form; only the total is carried to *Form IHT200.*

The notes at the top of the form tell you the order in which you should list the holdings. See chapter 4 for the method of valuing the holdings.

Column 1 asks for the name of the company and types of shares, e.g. the type of share, stock or unit trust, and its nominal value, e.g. 'ordinary 25p shares', '12½% unsecured loan stock' or 'managed fund units'.

Column 2 asks for the number of shares or amount of stock held.

The market price per share/unit should be included in Column 3. The figure in Column 4 is the value of the total holding, calculated by multiplying the number of shares/units in Column 2 by the price in Column 3.

Any dividends or interest due at death should be included in Column 5.

Supplementary page D12 Land, Buildings and Interests in Land
(see page 84 for completed example, Edward John Scott's estate)

Complete this form if the deceased owned any land; only the total amount will be carried to *Form IHT200*.

You should use separate supplementary pages if there was any land owned in Scotland or Northern Ireland. Either ask the Probate Registry for another form or photocopy the original.

The notes at the top tell you what to put in each column. If the property is let, attach copies of the tenancy agreements described in Column D.

Column F asks for the 'Open Market Value'; do not deduct the amount of any mortgage which has been or will need to be repaid. If the deceased owned, for example, the house in his or her sole name, record the gross value of the entire property, even if the spouse or someone else is claiming an interest in part of it. If the deceased was a joint owner of the property, you need only include the value of the deceased's share in Column F (in the example of Michael Stephen Brown's estate on page 84, both he and his wife, Frances Brown, owned the house as beneficial joint tenants—the deceased's half share in the house passes to his wife by survivorship).

At the Probate Registry

About three weeks after sending the probate forms, as set out in the flowcharts, the executors will be contacted with a time and date for an interview. All executors need to attend in order to swear an oath, which is needed to apply for the grant of probate. They will also need to produce the testator's original Will. Where the executors have completed a *Form IHT205*, this is signed at the Probate Registry interview.

Probate fees must be paid at this interview. It may therefore be necessary for executors to arrange for a loan or overdraft to pay these fees and the IHT due on the issue of the grant. Probate fees may be paid by cheque, banker's draft, postal order or in cash. On personal applications, the probate fee is currently £130, unless the net estate is less than £5,000, in which case no probate fee is payable for the grant.

At the interview, the executors will be asked to swear that the information on the oath and the Inland Revenue account is correct. It is a good idea to take back-up files to verify facts and figures. If all the information is exactly as the executors have previously submitted, they are asked to sign the account, swear to the facts set out in the oath, which refers to the Will and put their signatures on the Will. Then the commissioner handling the case adds his or her signature to the oath and Will. The executors may then order as many copies of the grant of probate, each bearing the court's seal, as are necessary to notify all the parties first informed of the death with copies of the death certificate. Copies currently cost £1 each. If there are further questions before the grant can be issued, the executors could be asked to return to the Registry for another interview.

In the case of an intestacy, the grant issued is a 'grant of letters of administration'. The administrator should order as many copies of the grant as are necessary, as above.

If there is no inheritance tax due, the grant will be issued almost immediately. Assuming there are no further questions, the grant of probate with a copy of the Will attached and the copies of the grant will arrive by post. The grant is proof to the public that the executors can realise the deceased's assets, collect from the deceased's debtors and distribute the assets as determined by the Will. Both the Will and the grant of probate are public documents.

The executors can now send a grant of probate to all parties that first received the death certificate, requesting whatever money is due to be sent to the executors. This money is deposited into the executors' bank account, from which debts of the deceased are paid.

Inheritance tax

The executors can calculate the tax themselves by working through the worksheet *IHT/WS*, and completing forms *IHT200* and *D18* accordingly. If the executors are not sure how to complete *Form IHT200*, the CTO helpline (tel: 0115 974 2400) can be contacted for assistance in completing the form.

If the executors do not wish to calculate the tax, the CTO will do this for them (see flowcharts for details).

The Inland Revenue exempts all property left to the surviving spouse or to charity and the first £234,000 of the estate not left to the spouse or charity. The excess bears tax at 40 per cent. The inheritance tax owed on buildings or land, a business or a share in a business, shares giving a controlling interest in a quoted company and some unquoted shares can, with prior approval, be paid in ten equal annual instalments (although interest is payable on these instalments if the asset is land or buildings). Inheritance tax on other assets must be paid before the grant of probate can be issued and interest is charged on any inheritance tax out-standing from the end of the sixth month after the death (except where it is being paid by non-interest bearing instalments).

Changes to the amount of inheritance tax

Even after probate has been granted, the Inland Revenue may ask further questions about the assets and liabilities of the estate, and values may have to be negotiated. For example, the Inland Revenue may challenge the value reported on *Form IHT200* for

Highlight

The IHT due on the application for the grant must be paid to the CTO prior to the issue of the grant by the Probate Registry.

a house or for unquoted shares. This could result in more inheritance tax being payable.

If the executors discover an asset or debt of the deceased which they did not know about before they applied for probate, they must report it to the Inland Revenue as soon as possible after its discovery. This may also change the amount of inheritance tax payable.

Once the inheritance tax position has been settled, the executors should ask the Inland Revenue for *Form 30*, an application to be discharged from further inheritance tax. Two copies completed and signed by the executors are needed by the Inland Revenue. One copy is returned certifying that no further inheritance tax is payable. The executors can then distribute the estate. However, if any further assets come to light subsequently, these too will need to be reported to the Inland Revenue, as the discharge from inheritance tax would not cover them.

Raising money to pay inheritance tax and the probate fee

Because an executor cannot draw on the funds in the deceased's bank account until he or she can show entitlement by producing the grant, the executor may need to borrow the necessary funds to pay inheritance tax and the probate fee. There are, however, some assets which an institution may be willing to release before the grant of probate is available, in order to pay the inheritance tax, and some assets that may be realised without producing the grant. The tax may be covered, or partly covered, from such sources as an alternative to borrowing. The following are assets which the executors may be able to use in this way.

1. **National Savings.** If the deceased had a National Savings account, National Savings certificates or Premium Bonds, National Savings may issue a cheque in favour of the Inland Revenue to cover the inheritance tax payable on the estate or part of it. The executors should explain to the Probate Registry at their interview that they would like to use funds of the deceased's National Savings account to pay the tax. The Registry will issue a note stating that the executors have made a personal application and showing the amount of probate fees and inheritance tax payable.

The Registry then sends this note to the relevant National Savings office, which will send the cheque for the tax and the probate fee to the Probate Registry directly. Any remaining balance on the deceased's National Savings account will be paid to the executors and any remaining National Savings certificates and Premium Bonds can be encashed once the grant has been obtained.

2. **Funds payable to others without grant of probate** (see *Is a grant of probate necessary?* in chapter 3). Consider utilising funds from nominated property, joint property or lump-sum death benefits from pension funds, life assurance companies and friendly societies which have been written in trust for another person. However, such funds or assets would belong to the person to whom they are payable, rather than to the estate, and the executors would need to borrow from that person if they wished to use those funds to pay the inheritance tax.

3. **Pension funds and friendly societies.** Funds of up to £5,000 from some pension funds and friendly societies.

4. **Building society or Girobank.** Building societies and the Girobank are often willing to release money to pay inheritance tax and the probate fee, but they may want to send the money direct to the Inland Revenue and HM Paymaster General to ensure that it is used for this purpose. The Girobank may be willing to lend the executors a sum up to the balance on the deceased's account to pay inheritance tax and the probate fee.

5. **Other assets.** Furniture and other personal possessions of the deceased may be sold by executors, who are entitled to sell the assets of the estate from the date of death, but not administrators, who are only entitled to do so once they have the grant of letters of administration.

6. **Stocks and shares.** If held through a stockbroker's nominee company.

If insufficient assets are realisable before the grant is issued, the executors will have to borrow the money to pay the inheritance tax. Some sources might include:

Highlight

If insufficient assets are realisable before the grant is issued, the executors will have to borrow the money to pay the inheritance tax.

1. **Loan from the deceased's bank.** A bank will normally make a loan to the executors, although a fee will be payable based on the size of the loan and, of course, interest will be charged. The executors may claim income tax relief on the interest payment for the first year of the administration in respect of a loan for the inheritance tax payable on personal property.

2. **Loan from a beneficiary.** A beneficiary may be able and willing to lend the money to the estate to pay the inheritance tax, particularly if the bank interest and fee would be paid out of cash that he or she would otherwise receive.

Administering an estate

6

Distribution of gifts and legacies —

To satisfy any debts of the estate, it is the assets forming part of the residuary estate that are used first. If there are still outstanding debts when the residuary estate has been used up, cash legacies are reduced proportionately to meet the debt. If there are unpaid debts outstanding, specific items left as legacies under the Will need to be sold. Once all the debts are paid and the assets are all accounted for and collected the executors are in a position to distribute the estate in accordance with the Will.

As each personal effect, gift and legacy of money is distributed to the beneficiaries of the estate, the executors should ask each beneficiary to sign a receipt. The receipt should record the amount of money or description of the gift, the names of the executors, the name and signature of the beneficiary and the date. The beneficiary should keep a copy of the receipt. The Will may contain a clause saying that, if there is a gift to a child, his or her parent or guardian can sign the receipt. Otherwise, gifts to minors should be invested by the executor in an account until the child reaches 18.

Transfer of assets

If assets are to be transferred to a beneficiary (rather than being sold and the proceeds paid to him or her), the method of transfer will differ according to the asset. Household and personal effects may be physically handed over, without any legal paperwork.

Shares will need to be transferred using *Form Con 40*, available from legal stationers (see completed example on page 90). This should be completed and signed by all executors and sent to the registrar of the company, together with the share certificate and an office copy of the grant of probate. Alternatively, a stockbroker or bank would be able to prepare the stock transfer forms and send them to the registrars. If a shareholding is to be split between two or more beneficiaries, a separate form is needed for each beneficiary. No stamp duty is payable on the transfer of shares from executors to a beneficiary, provided that the certificate on the back of the form has been completed and signed by the executors. Where the shares are given in the Will as a specific legacy, the appropriate category to be inserted in the certificate is 'B', and if they are part of the residue, the appropriate category is 'E'. If the shares are registered in the name of a stockbroker's or bank's nominee company, the executors need not complete stock transfer forms but should write to the nominee company, giving it the name and address of the beneficiary of the shares and instructing it to hold the shares on behalf of the beneficiary in future.

If a house or flat is to be transferred to a beneficiary, the procedure differs according to whether the title is registered or unregistered. The document needed to transfer the ownership of the property is called an *assent*.

In the case of registered land title(s), you need to use Land Registry *Form AS1 Assent of whole of registered title(s),* available from legal stationers. If only part of the registered land title is being transferred, you will need to complete a *Form AS3*. The completed form needs to be signed by each executor in the presence of a witness and by the beneficiary to whom the property is being transferred (see example on page 92). The executors should then send it, together with an office copy of the grant of probate, the land certificate and the Land Registry fee to the Land Registry so they can register the new owner. The Land Registry fee will vary according to the value of the property, net of any outstanding mortgage (if it has not been repaid following the death). The current scale of fees for registering an assent is as follows:

Highlight

The document needed to transfer the ownership of the property is called an *assent*.

Value net of mortgage	Fee
£0 –£100,000	£40
£100,001–£200,000	£50
£200,001–£500,000	£70
£500,001–£1,000,000	£100
£1,000,001 and over	£200

If the land is unregistered the title deeds will consist of a number of deeds and documents including the deed (a *conveyance*) whereby the property was transferred to the deceased. In the case of unregistered land it is best to seek the advice of a solicitor as the title to the property would then have to be registered at the Land Registry as a first registration application.

Final accounts

The careful records that have been kept since the date of death should now be organised in a neat and easily-read format for approval by each beneficiary. A word of caution: for a period of sixth months following the grant of probate claims may be made under the Inheritance (Provision for Family and Dependants) Act 1975, for example by a member of the deceased's family who feels he or she has not been properly provided for in the Will. It is therefore wise not to distribute the residue of the estate until six months has passed. If such a claim is made the executors should seek the advice of a solicitor.

Highlight

After the beneficiaries have signed off on the accounts the estate is completed.

After the beneficiaries have signed off on the accounts the estate is completed. The executors' bank account can be closed and whatever money remains is given to the residuary beneficiary.

Paperwork should be kept on file for 12 years after final distribution. In the event that the deceased left someone a life interest in the estate, the paperwork should be kept for 12 years after the final distribution to whoever inherits after the death of the last person with a life interest.

Taxation of the estate

The estate will be liable to income tax and capital gains tax from the date of death to the date it has been fully administered. The estate will be assessed to income tax on all income received gross at the basic rate, but with no personal allowance. No further income tax will be payable if all income (e.g. bank interest, dividends, etc.) has been paid net of tax. The executors' annual exemption for capital gains tax is the same, for the tax year in which the death occurred and the following two years, as any individual's annual exemption (£7,200 for the tax year 2000/01). However, gains in an estate are taxed at 34%. Thus the executors should liaise with the beneficiaries before selling assets which are likely to make a taxable gain to see whether the capital gains tax can be reduced by using the beneficiaries' rates of tax and exemptions. If in doubt, the executors should seek professional advice. When the executors notify the Tax Inspector for the deceased's tax district of the death, the Inspector will send *Form 920* which asks for information as to who will be entitled to the residue of the estate, whether there will be any trust continuing after the estate has been wound up and whether the executor expects to receive any untaxed income or make any capital gains. On the basis of that form the Inspector will issue the correct tax returns to be filled in for the estate.

The executors will also need to issue a certificate of tax deduction (*Form R185 (Estate Income)*, also available from the tax office) to the beneficiary who is entitled to the residue of the estate. This form shows the gross income received by the estate during the tax year, the tax paid by the executors on that income and the resulting net figure. As long as the residue is not held in trust, the income of the estate is treated as the income of the beneficiary, who will report the income on his or her tax return, and *Form R185 (Estate Income)* is evidence that tax has already been paid on it. If the beneficiary is a non-taxpayer, he or she can reclaim the tax. If he or she is a higher rate taxpayer, he or she will be assessable to additional tax.

Succession on intestacy

If someone dies without leaving a Will, the order in which the various members of the family are entitled to share in the estate is illustrated in the flowchart shown below.

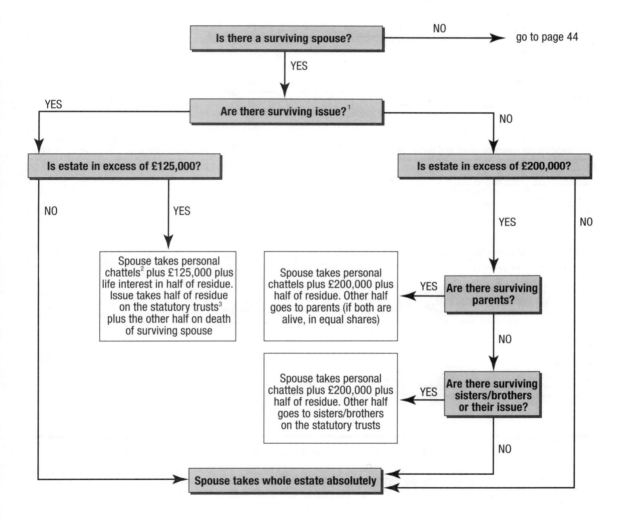

1 **'ISSUE'** Children, grandchildren or remoter lineal descendants of the intestate.

2 **'PERSONAL CHATTELS'** Under s.55 (1) (x) of the Administration of Estates Act 1925, 'personal chattels' includes: horses, motor cars, garden implements, domestic animals, furniture, linen, china, glass, books, pictures, musical and scientific instruments, jewellery, household and personal articles, food and drink, but does not include any chattels used at the date of death for business purposes nor money or securities.

3 **'THE STATUTORY TRUSTS'** Those children of the intestate who are alive at his or her death inherit in equal shares although if a child is under 18 he or she must reach the age of 18 or marry under that age in order to inherit. If any child dies before the intestate, leaving children of his or her own, those children (i.e. the intestate's grandchildren) will take *per stirpes* i.e. they will take their parents' share equally between them (provided they reach the age of 18 or marry under that age). If remoter issue predeceased the intestate leaving their own issue, this process would continue down the generations. References to the children of the intestate should be read as references to brothers, sisters, aunts or uncles as appropriate, where any of those classes are stated to inherit on the statutory trusts. See illustration of *per stirpes* distribution on page 44.

Succession on intestacy (continued)

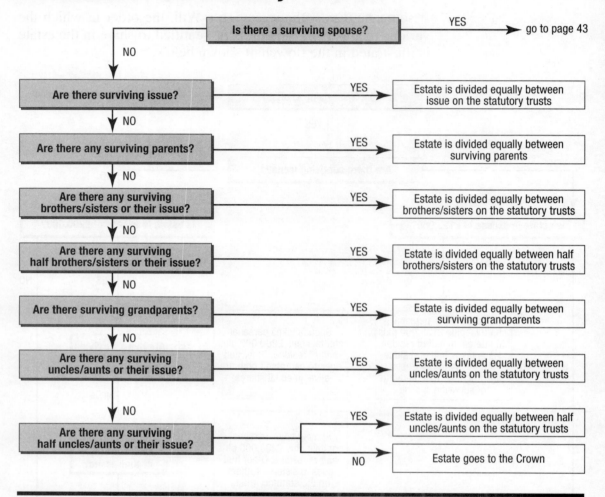

Is there a surviving spouse?	YES →	go to page 43

↓ NO

| **Are there surviving issue?** | YES → | Estate is divided equally between issue on the statutory trusts |

↓ NO

| **Are there any surviving parents?** | YES → | Estate is divided equally between surviving parents |

↓ NO

| **Are there any surviving brothers/sisters or their issue?** | YES → | Estate is divided equally between brothers/sisters on the statutory trusts |

↓ NO

| **Are there any surviving half brothers/sisters or their issue?** | YES → | Estate is divided equally between half brothers/sisters on the statutory trusts |

↓ NO

| **Are there surviving grandparents?** | YES → | Estate is divided equally between surviving grandparents |

↓ NO

| **Are there any surviving uncles/aunts or their issue?** | YES → | Estate is divided equally between uncles/aunts on the statutory trusts |

↓ NO

| **Are there any surviving half uncles/aunts or their issue?** | YES → | Estate is divided equally between half uncles/aunts on the statutory trusts |
| | NO → | Estate goes to the Crown |

Illustration of *per stirpes* distribution (ignoring inheritance tax)

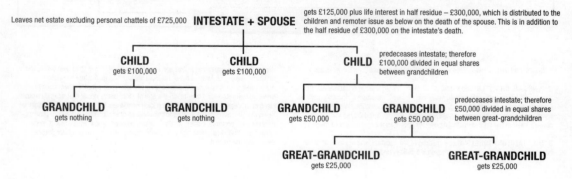

Leaves net estate excluding personal chattels of £725,000 **INTESTATE + SPOUSE** gets £125,000 plus life interest in half residue – £300,000, which is distributed to the children and remoter issue as below on the death of the spouse. This is in addition to the half residue of £300,000 on the intestate's death.

CHILD gets £100,000

CHILD gets £100,000

CHILD predeceases intestate; therefore £100,000 divided in equal shares between grandchildren

GRANDCHILD gets nothing

GRANDCHILD gets nothing

GRANDCHILD gets £50,000

GRANDCHILD gets £50,000 predeceases intestate; therefore £50,000 divided in equal shares between great-grandchildren

GREAT-GRANDCHILD gets £25,000

GREAT-GRANDCHILD gets £25,000

Glossary of useful terms

A-G

Administrators – the personal representatives appointed when the deceased dies intestate or where there are no executors able or willing to act.

Assent – document whereby land or buildings are transferred to a beneficiary of an estate.

Beneficial joint tenants – joint holders of property who are treated as a single unit.

Beneficial tenants in common – joint holders of property with individual shares in the property.

Beneficiary – a person who receives all or part of an estate under a Will or intestacy. A beneficiary may also be the person who receives payment from a life insurance policy or a trust.

Estate – all the property belonging to a person when he or she dies.

Executor/executrix – a personal representative who has been appointed by a valid Will.

Grant of letters of administration – the official document obtained by administrators of an estate on an administration intestacy showing that they have the legal authority to deal with the deceased's property.

G-M

Grant of letters of administration with Will annexed – the official document obtained by administrators where there is a Will, but the executors named are unwilling or unable to act, showing they have the legal authority to deal with the deceased's property.

Grant of probate – the official document obtained by executors which shows that they have the legal authority to deal with the deceased's property.

Informant – the person who registers the death.

Inheritance tax – a tax on the value of a person's estate on death and in some cases on gifts during the person's lifetime.

Insolvent estate – an estate where the debts of the deceased and other liabilities of the estate, including funeral and administration expenses, exceed the assets of the estate.

Intestacy rules – the rules which govern the distribution of property belonging to a person who dies intestate.

Intestate – the deceased is intestate if he or she dies without leaving a valid Will.

Issue – child, grandchild or more remote descendant including children born either within or outside marriage, and adopted children.

Joint tenancy – a way of holding property jointly whereby when one of the joint owners dies, his or her share passes automatically to the other joint owner.

Legatee – a person who receives a gift under a Will.

Life interest – entitlement to income for life under a trust. When the person with a life interest dies, the property is not distributed in accordance with his Will or intestacy but is dealt with in accordance with the Will of the person who set up the trust.

Minor – person aged under 18.

Nominated property – property which the deceased has nominated a particular person to receive after his death (certain National Savings investments and government stock only).

P-U

Personal representatives – executors or administrators.

Power reserved letter – a letter issued by the Probate Registry which an executor signs in order to renounce his duties as executor for the time being.

Registered land – land or buildings, the ownership of which is registered at HM Land Registry.

Residuary legatee – a person who receives all or part of the residue of a person's estate.

Residue – the remainder of a person's estate after paying all the debts, liabilities, taxes, costs and legacies.

Tenancy-in-common – way of holding property jointly whereby when one of the joint owners dies, his or her share of the property forms part of his or her estate.

Testator/Testatrix – a person who makes a Will.

Title – ownership.

Trust – a formal legal arrangement whereby property is held by and under the control of one person (a 'trustee') for the benefit of another (a 'beneficiary').

Unregistered land – land or buildings, the ownership of which is not registered at HM Land Registry.

Appendices

		Page
1	Probate Registries	52
2	Example letter to deceased's mortgage lender	57
3	Example letter to deceased's bank	58

APPENDIX 1

PROBATE REGISTRIES AND LOCAL OFFICES

Controlling Probate offices are open 9.30 a.m.–4.00 p.m. Opening times for local offices may be different. You can get addresses and hours for local offices by calling the Probate Registries.

Controlling Probate Registry	Local Offices
Bangor Council Offices Ffordd Gwynedd LL57 1DT Tel. 01248 362410	Rhyl Wrexham
Birmingham The Priory Courts 33 Bull Street Lichfield B4 6DU Tel. 0121 681 3400/3414	Coventry Birmingham Kidderminster Northampton Wolverhampton
Bodmin Market Street PL31 2JW Tel. 01208 72279	Truro Penzance Plymouth
Brighton William St BN2 2LG. Tel. 01273 684071	Chichester Crawley Hastings
Bristol The Crescent Centre Temple Back BS1 6EP Tel. 0117 927 3915/926 4619	Bath Weston-Super-Mare

Controlling Probate Registry	Local Offices
Cardiff Probate Registry of Wales PO Box 474 2 Park Street Cardiff CF1 1TB Tel. 029 2037 6479	Bridgend Newport Pontypridd
Carlisle Courts of Justice Earl Street Carlisle CA1 1DJ Tel. 01228 21751	Workington
Carthmarthen 14 King Street Dyfed SA31 1BL Tel. 01267 236238	Aberystwyth Haverfordwest Swansea
Chester 5th Floor, Hamilton House Hamilton Place CH1 2DA Tel. 01244 345082	
Exeter Finance House Barnfield Road Exeter EX1 1QR Tel. 01392 274515	Barnstaple Newton Abbot Taunton Yeovil Plymouth
Gloucester 2nd Floor, Combined Court Building Kimbrose Way Gloucester GL1 2DG Tel. 01452 522585	Cheltenham Hereford Worcester
Ipswich Level 3 Haven House 17 Lower Brook Street IP4 1DN Tel. 01473 253724/259261	Chelmsford Colchester

Controlling Probate Registry	Local Offices
Lancaster Mitre House Church Street. LA1 1HE Tel. 01524 36625	Barrow-in-Furness Blackpool Preston
Leeds 3rd Floor Coronet House Queen Street LS1 2BA Tel. 0113 243 1505	Bradford Harrogate Huddersfield Wakefield
Leicester 5th Floor Leicester House Lee Circle LE1 3RE Tel. 0116 253 8558	Bedford Kettering
Lincoln Mill House Brayford Side North LN1 1YW Tel. 01522 523648	Grimsby
Liverpool The Queen Elizabeth II Law Courts Derby Square Liverpool L2 1XA Tel. 0151 236 8264	Southport St. Helens Wallasey
London **Principal Registry** Family Division First Avenue House 42–49 High Holborn London WC1V 6NP Tel. 020 7947 6939 Personal enquiries Room 83	Croydon Edmonton Harlow Kingston Luton Southend-on-Sea Woolwich

Controlling Probate Registry	**Local Offices**
Maidstone The Law Courts Baker Road ME16 8EW Tel. 01622 202048	Canterbury Chatham Folkestone Tunbridge Wells
Manchester 9th Floor Astley House 23 Quay Street M3 4AT Tel. 0161 834 4319	Bolton Nelson Oldham Stockport Warrington Wigan
Middlesbrough Combined Court Centre Russell Street Middlesbrough Cleveland TS1 2AE Tel. 01642 340001	Darlington Durham
Newcastle-upon-Tyne 2nd Floor Plummer House Croft Street NE1 6NP Tel. 0191 261 8383	Morpeth Sunderland
Norwich Combined Court Building The Law Courts Bishopsgate Norwich NR3 1UR Tel. 01603 761776	Lowestoft
Nottingham Butt Dyke House 33 Park Row Nottingham NG1 6GR Tel. 0115 941 4288	Derby Mansfield

Controlling Probate Registry	**Local Offices**
Oxford 10A New Road OX1 1LY Tel. 01865 241163	Reading Slough Swindon Aylesbury High Wycombe
Peterborough Crown Buildings Rivergate PE1 1EJ Tel. 01733 62802	Cambridge Kings Lynn
Sheffield PO Box 832 The Law Courts 50 West Bar Sheffield S3 8YR Tel. 0114 272 2596	Chesterfield Doncaster
Stoke-on-Trent Combined Court Centre Bethesda Street Hanley ST1 3BP Tel. 01782 854065	Crewe Shrewsbury Stafford
Winchester 4th Floor Cromwell House Andover Road SO23 7EW Tel. 01962 863771 (2 lines)	Basingstoke Bournemouth Dorchester Guildford Newport I.O.W. Portsmouth Salisbury Southampton
York Duncombe Place YO1 2EA Tel. 01904 624210	Hull Scarborough

Windmill Cottage
Petworth
West Sussex TN20 7XP

27th May 2000

Dear Sirs

Patricia Lacey
2 Allan Gardens
Chichester PO7 2X5
Roll number: A/678123

I am an executor of the estate of Patricia Lacey, who died on 19th May 2000. My two co-executors are Louise Jones of 102 Oakley Road, Guildford, Surrey, G9 5TT and Mark Robinson of 52 Mulford Avenue, Winchester, SO23 9XT. I enclose a copy of the death certificate, which I would be grateful if you would return to me once you have noted the details.

Please let me know the amount of capital outstanding on the above mortgage and the amount of interest due at the date of death.

Miss Lacey held an endowment policy with County Insurance reference number 3579/246A. Please let me know what sum is payable under the policy following her death and if there will be any surplus remaining after repayment.

Yours faithfully,

David Chambers

David Chambers

17 Arundel Way
Bristol BS8 3JQ

30th July 2000

Dear Sirs

Edward John Scott, deceased
Account number: 00034567

I am an executor of the estate of my father, the late Edward John Scott, who died on 27 July 2000. My co-executor is my sister, Rosemary Jane Rayner, who lives at 98 Churchill Road, Swindon, SN9 4SZ. I enclose a copy of the death certificate, which I should be grateful if you would return once you have noted the details.

Please would you:

1.   Put an immediate stop on all unpaid cheques and standing orders from the above account.

2.   Let me know the balance on the account at the date of death and, as a separate figure, any interest accrued but not credited up to that date.

3.   Send me a list of any deeds and documents you are holding on Mr. Scott's behalf.

4.   Let me know the amount of interest paid during the current tax year up to the date of death, whether it was paid gross or net and the amount of any tax deducted.

My sister and I wish to open an executor's account and I should be grateful if you would send me the appropriate forms for us to sign in order to do that.

Yours faithfully,

Melanie Scott

Melanie Scott

The forms in this Guide

This guide contains completed examples of the following forms for reference when completing your own. You should obtain copies of the forms you need from your local Probate Registry, the Capital Taxes Office or a legal stationer, as appropriate.

	Form No.	Form name	Page
	PA1	Probate application	60
	IHT200	Full account for personal applicants	64
		Supplementary pages:	
	D1	The Will	72
	D17	Continuation sheet for additional information	73
Available from Probate Registry/ Capital Taxes Office	D18	Probate summary	74
	D3	Gifts and other transfers of value	75
	D4	Joint and nominated assets	77
	D7	Stocks and shares	79
	D9	Life insurance and annuities	81
	D10	Household and personal goods	83
	D12	Land, buildings and interests in land	84
	IHT205	Short form for personal applicants	86
Available from legal stationers	Con 40	Stock transfer form	91
	AS1	Assent of whole of registered title(s)	93

Completed example of Form PA1 Probate application

Probate application form

Please read the booklet HOW TO OBTAIN PROBATE

USE CAPITAL LETTERS

This Column is for official use

At which Probate Registry or local office do you want to be interviewed?
(See pages 6-12 of the booklet)

SECTION 1

BRISTOL PROBATE REGISTRY

Details of the deceased

SECTION 2

True Name

1 Surname — SCOTT

2 Fornames — EDWARD JOHN

3 Are any assets held in another name?

Answer YES or NO — NO

If YES, what are the assets?

Alias

and in what name(s) are they held?

Address

F/O

4 Address of the deceased — 16 JAMES COURT

BATH BA7 4NH

D/C district & no

5 Occupation of deceased at time of death. State RETIRED or OF NO OCCUPATION if applicable — SALES MANAGER

L.S.A.

D.B.F.

6 Date of death — 27TH JULY 1999   Age   55

7 Date of birth — 2ND FEBRUARY 1944

8 TICK the **legal** marital status of the deceased, and give dates where appropriate

Bachelor ☐
Spinster ☐
Widowed ☐
Married ☑ date 4/5/91
Divorced ☐ date _____
Legally separated ☐ date _____

FORM PA1 (3/95)

(Continued on next page)

Completed example of Form PA1 Probate application (continued)

This Column is for official use

SECTION 3 — The Will

1 Did the deceased leave a will?
PLEASE NOTE that a will may not necessarily be a formal document

Answer YES or NO — **YES**

Date of will/codicil

2 Is there anyone under 18 years old who receives a gift in the will?

Answer YES or NO — **NO**

3 Are there any executors named in the will?

Answer YES or NO — **YES**

Reason A,B,C,D

4 Give the name(s) of those executors who are not applying and reason A, B, C or D

NOT APPLICABLE

A - died before the deceased
B - died after the deceased
C - does not wish to apply
D - does not wish to apply now but may later

SECTION 4 — Relatives of the deceased

1 Give the **number** of relatives, over 18 and under 18 years old in each category
If none cross through each box
PLEASE NOTE survived means they were alive when the deceased died

NUMBER — If none cross through each box	over 18	under 18
Sons or daughters who survived the deceased	2	
Sons or daughters who did not survive the deceased	0	
Their children who survived the deceased	1	
Parents who survived the deceased	1	
Brothers or sisters who survived the deceased	0	
Brothers or sisters who did not survive the deceased		
Their children who survived the deceased	0	
Grandparents who survived the deceased		

2 Was the deceased adopted?

Answer YES or NO — **NO**

3 Has any relative of the deceased been adopted?

Answer YES or NO — **NO**

If YES give their name(s) and relationship(s) to the deceased:

Answer questions 4, 5 and 6 only if the deceased died before 4th April 1988 or left a will or codicil dated before that date.

4 Was the deceased illegitimate?

Answer YES or NO

5 Did the deceased leave any illegitimate sons or daughters?

Answer YES or NO

6 Did the deceased have any illegitimate sons or daughters who died leaving children of their own?

Answer YES or NO

(Continued on next page)

SECTION 5   Details of applicant

This Column is
for official use

PLEASE NOTE that the grant will normally
be sent to the first applicant

Tick correct box

1 Title   Mr ☐   Mrs ☐   Miss ✓   I.T.W.C.

2 Forenames   MELANIE

3 Surname   SCOTT

4 Address   17 ARUNDEL WAY

BRISTOL

Postcode   BS8 3JQ

5 Occupation/marital status   ACCOUNTANT / SINGLE

6 Tel. No.   at home 0117 123456   at work 0117 654321

7 Are you related to the deceased?   Answer YES or NO   YES

8 If YES what is your relationship in law?   DAUGHTER

9 Name and address of any surviving husband or wife of the deceased, unless stated above   JULIA ANNE SCOTT

If there are any other applicants give their details as shown above

Details of other applicants who wish to be named in the grant of administration and attend the interview

ROSEMARY JANE RAYNER

98 CHURCHILL ROAD

SWINDON SN9 4SZ

OCCUPATION: TEACHER

MARITAL STATUS: MARRIED

TELEPHONE NO.(HOME): 01793 355688

TELEPHONE NO.(WORK): 01793 111666

When you return this form you MUST also send:

- **The original death certificate**
- **The original will (if there is one)**
- **The account of the estate (IHT200 or IHT 205)**

Now please refer to the booklet for the address to which you should send your application

(Continued on next page)

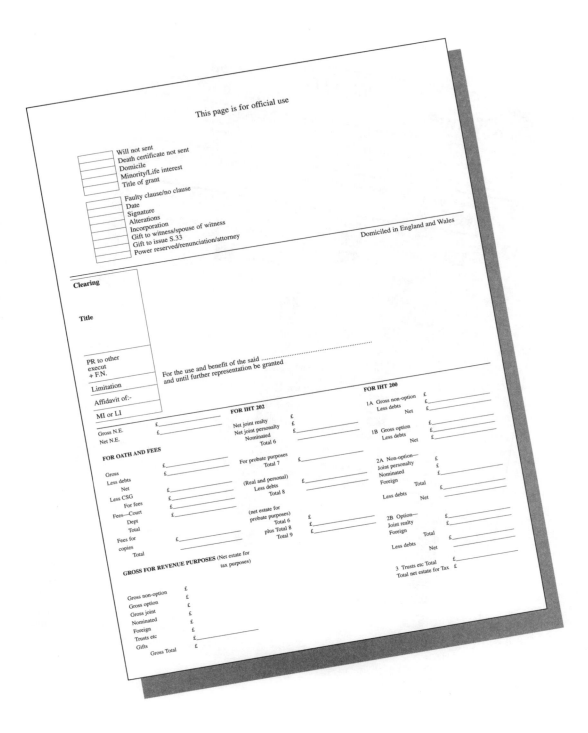

This page is for official use

Will not sent
Death certificate not sent
Domicile
Minority/Life interest
Title of grant

Faulty clause/no clause
Date
Signature
Alterations
Incorporation
Gift to witness/spouse of witness
Gift to issue S.33
Power reserved/renunciation/attorney

Domiciled in England and Wales

Clearing

Title

PR to other
execut
+ F.N.

Limitation

Affidavit of:-

MI or LI

Gross N.E.   £
Net N.E.   £

For the use and benefit of the said ....
and until further representation be granted

FOR IHT 200

1A Gross non-option   £
   Less debts   £
         Net   £

1B Gross option   £
   Less debts   £
         Net   £

FOR IHT 202

Net joint realty   £
Net joint personalty   £
Nominated   £
         Total 6

For probate purposes   £
         Total 7

(Real and personal)   £
   Less debts
         Total 8

(net estate for   £
probate purposes)   £
   Total 6   £
   plus Total 8
         Total 9

2A Non-option—   £
   Joint personalty   £
   Nominated
   Foreign   Total   £
   Less debts   Net   £

2B Option—   £
   Joint realty   £
   Foreign   Total   £
   Less debts   Net   £

3 Trusts etc Total   £
Total net estate for Tax £

FOR OATH AND FEES

Gross   £
Less debts   £
   Net   £
Less CSG   £
   For fees   £
Fees—Court   £
   Dept
   Total
Fees for   £
copies
   Total

GROSS FOR REVENUE PURPOSES (Net estate for tax purposes)

Gross non-option   £
Gross option   £
Gross joint   £
Nominated   £
Foreign   £
Trusts etc   £
Gifts   £
   Gross Total

Completed example of Form IHT200
Full account for personal applicants

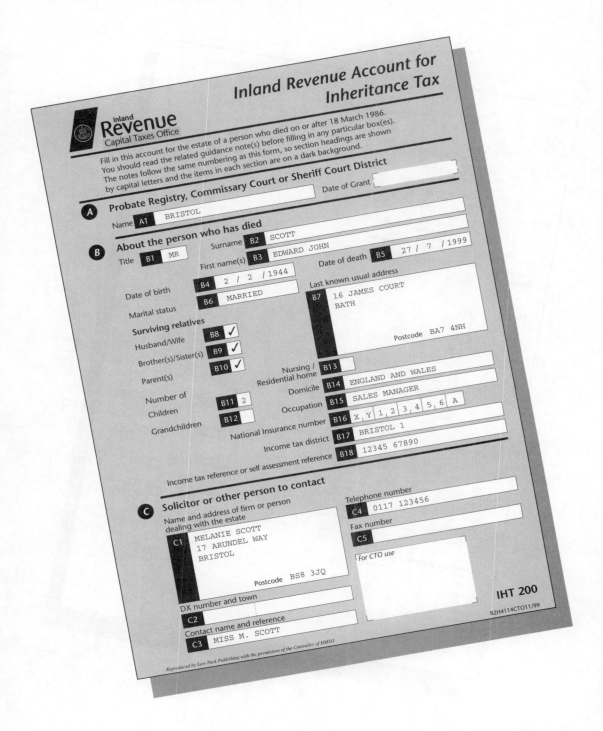

Inland Revenue Account for Inheritance Tax

Inland Revenue Capital Taxes Office

Fill in this account for the estate of a person who died on or after 18 March 1986. You should read the related guidance note(s) before filling in any particular box(es). The notes follow the same numbering as this form, so section headings are shown by capital letters and the items in each section are on a dark background.

A Probate Registry, Commissary Court or Sheriff Court District

Date of Grant

Name **A1** BRISTOL

B About the person who has died

Title **B1** MR

Surname **B2** SCOTT

First name(s) **B3** EDWARD JOHN

Date of death **B5** 27 / 7 / 1999

Date of birth **B4** 2 / 2 / 1944

Marital status **B6** MARRIED

Last known usual address **B7** 16 JAMES COURT BATH

Postcode BA7 4NH

Surviving relatives

Husband/Wife **B8** ✓

Brother(s)/Sister(s) **B9** ✓

Parent(s) **B10** ✓

Nursing / Residential home **B13**

Domicile **B14** ENGLAND AND WALES

Number of Children **B11** 2

Occupation **B15** SALES MANAGER

Grandchildren **B12**

National Insurance number **B16** X Y 1 2 3 4 5 6 A

Income tax district **B17** BRISTOL 1

Income tax reference or self assessment reference **B18** 12345 67890

C Solicitor or other person to contact

Name and address of firm or person dealing with the estate

C1 MELANIE SCOTT 17 ARUNDEL WAY BRISTOL

Postcode BS8 3JQ

Telephone number **C4** 0117 123456

Fax number **C5**

For CTO use

DX number and town **C2**

Contact name and reference **C3** MISS M. SCOTT

IHT 200

R2H4114CTO11/99

Reproduced by Law Pack Publishing with the permission of the Controller of HMSO

(Continued on next page)

64

Completed example of Form IHT200
Full account for personal applicants (continued)

D Supplementary pages

You must answer all of the questions in this section. You should read the notes starting at page 10 of form IHT 210 before answering the questions.

If you answer "Yes" to a question you will need to fill in the supplementary page shown. If you do not have all the supplementary pages you need you should telephone our Orderline on 0845 2341000.

	Question	No	Yes	Page
		☐	✓	D1
		✓	☐	D2
The Will	Did the deceased leave a Will?			
Domicile outside the United Kingdom	Was the deceased domiciled outside the UK at the date of death?	☐	✓	D3
Gifts and other transfers of value	Did the deceased make any gift or any other transfer of value on or after 18 March 1986?	☐	✓	D4
Joint assets	Did the deceased hold any asset(s) in joint names with another person?	✓	☐	D4
Nominated assets	Did the deceased, at any time during their lifetime, give written instructions (usually called a "nomination") that any asset was to pass to a particular person on their death?	✓	☐	D5
Assets held in trust	Did the deceased have any right to any benefit from any assets held in trust or in a settlement at the date of death?	✓	☐	D6
Pensions	Did the deceased have provision for a pension, other than the State Pension, from employers, a personal pension policy or other provisions made for retirement?	☐	✓	D7
Stocks and shares	Did the deceased own any stocks or shares?	✓	☐	D8
Debts due to the estate	Did the deceased lend any money, either on mortgage or by personal loan, that had not been repaid by the date of death?	☐	✓	D9
Life insurance and annuities	Did the deceased pay any premiums on any life insurance policies or annuities which are payable to either the estate or to someone else or which continue after death?	☐	✓	D10
Household and personal goods	Did the deceased own any household goods or other personal possessions?	✓	☐	D11
Interest in another estate	Did the deceased have a right to a legacy or a share of an estate of someone who died before them, but which they had not received before they died?	☐	✓	D12
Land, buildings and interests in land	Did the deceased own any land or buildings in the UK?	✓	☐	D13
Agricultural relief	Are you deducting agricultural relief?	✓	☐	D14
Business interests	Did the deceased own all or part of a business or were they a partner in a business?	✓	☐	D14
Business relief	Are you deducting business relief?	✓	☐	D15
Foreign assets	Did the deceased own any assets outside the UK?	✓	☐	D16
Debts owed by the estate	Are you claiming a deduction against the estate for any money that the deceased had borrowed from relatives, close friends, or trustees, or other loans, overdrafts or guarantee debts?			

2

(Continued on next page)

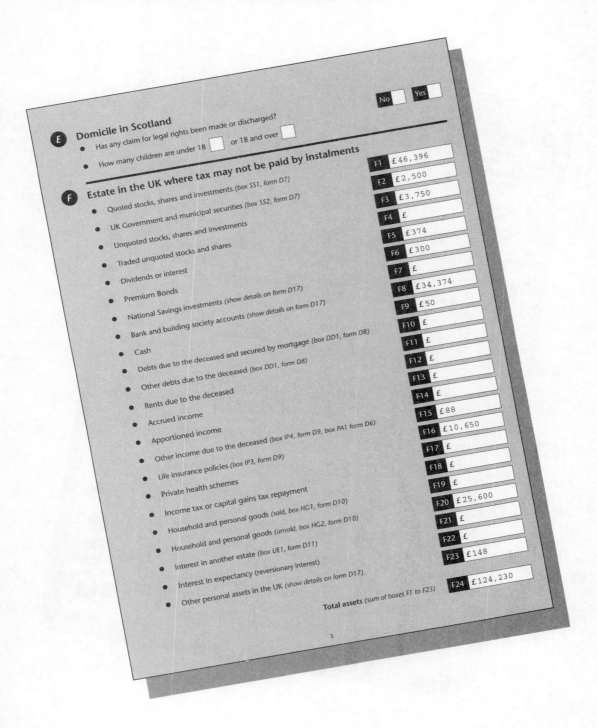

No | Yes

E **Domicile in Scotland**

- Has any claim for legal rights been made or discharged?
- How many children are under 18 [ ] or 18 and over [ ]

F **Estate in the UK where tax may not be paid by instalments**

Quoted stocks, shares and investments *(box SS1, form D7)*	F1 £46,396
UK Government and municipal securities *(box SS2, form D7)*	F2 £2,500
Unquoted stocks, shares and investments	F3 £3,750
Traded unquoted stocks and shares	F4 £
Dividends or interest	F5 £374
Premium Bonds	F6 £300
National Savings investments *(show details on form D17)*	F7 £
Bank and building society accounts *(show details on form D17)*	F8 £34,374
Cash	F9 £50
Debts due to the deceased and secured by mortgage *(box DD1, form D8)*	F10 £
Other debts due to the deceased *(box DD1, form D8)*	F11 £
Rents due to the deceased	F12 £
Accrued income	F13 £
Apportioned income	F14 £
Other income due to the deceased *(box IP4, form D9, box PA1 form D6)*	F15 £88
Life insurance policies *(box IP3, form D9)*	F16 £10,650
Private health schemes	F17 £
Income tax or capital gains tax repayment	F18 £
Household and personal goods *(sold, box HG1, form D10)*	F19 £
Household and personal goods *(unsold, box HG2, form D10)*	F20 £25,600
Interest in another estate *(box UE1, form D11)*	F21 £
Interest in expectancy *(reversionary interest)*	F22 £
Other personal assets in the UK *(show details on form D17)*	F23 £148
Total assets *(sum of boxes F1 to F23)*	F24 £124,230

3

(Continued on next page)

Completed example of Form IHT200
Full account for personal applicants (continued)

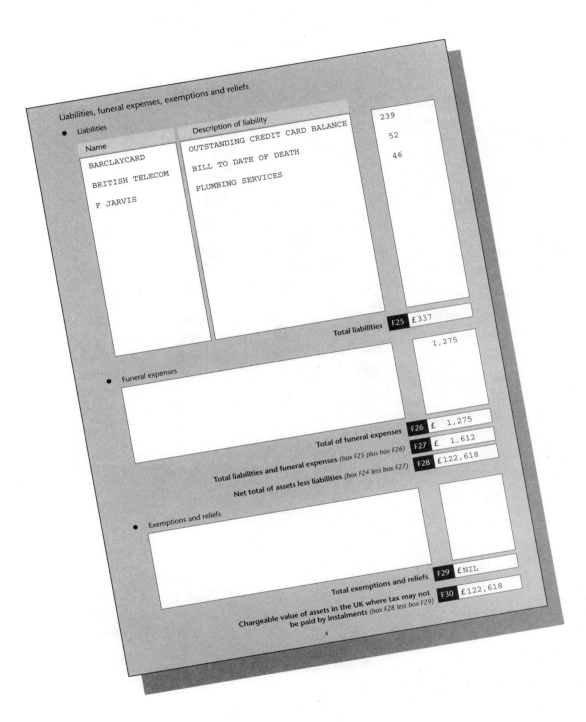

Liabilities, funeral expenses, exemptions and reliefs

● Liabilities

Name	Description of liability	
BARCLAYCARD	OUTSTANDING CREDIT CARD BALANCE	239
BRITISH TELECOM	BILL TO DATE OF DEATH	52
F JARVIS	PLUMBING SERVICES	46

Total liabilities **F25** £337

● Funeral expenses

1,275

Total of funeral expenses **F26** £ 1,275

Total liabilities and funeral expenses *(box F25 plus box F26)* **F27** £ 1,612

Net total of assets less liabilities *(box F24 less box F27)* **F28** £122,618

● Exemptions and reliefs

Total exemptions and reliefs **F29** £NIL

Chargeable value of assets in the UK where tax may not be paid by instalments *(box F28 less box F29)* **F30** £122,618

4

(Continued on next page)

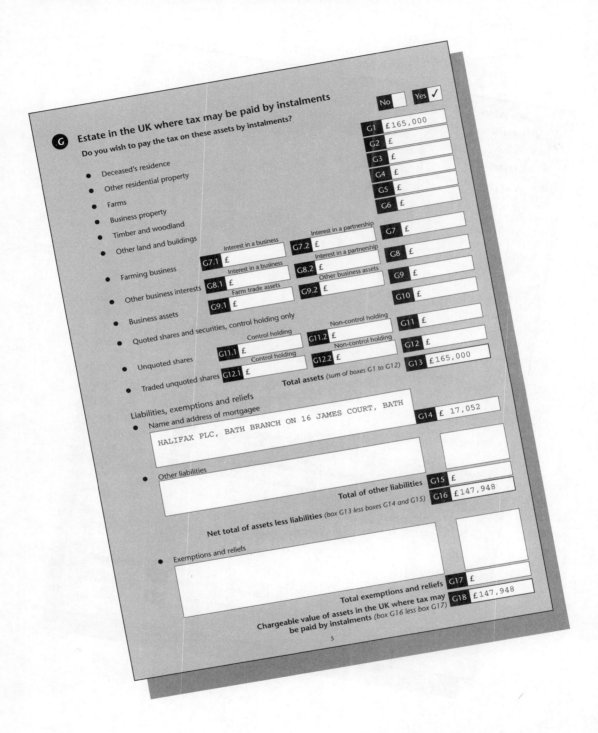

G **Estate in the UK where tax may be paid by instalments**

No ☐   Yes ✓

Do you wish to pay the tax on these assets by instalments?

- Deceased's residence — G1 £165,000
- Other residential property — G2 £
- Farms — G3 £
- Business property — G4 £
- Timber and woodland — G5 £
- Other land and buildings — G6 £
- Farming business — G7 £
  - Interest in a business G7.1 £
  - Interest in a partnership G7.2 £
- Other business interests — G8 £
  - Interest in a business G8.1 £
  - Interest in a partnership G8.2 £
- Business assets — G9 £
  - Farm trade assets G9.1 £
  - Other business assets G9.2 £
- Quoted shares and securities, control holding only — G10 £
- Unquoted shares — G11 £
  - Control holding G11.1 £
  - Non-control holding G11.2 £
- Traded unquoted shares — G12 £
  - Control holding G12.1 £
  - Non-control holding G12.2 £

Total assets *(sum of boxes G1 to G12)* G13 £165,000

Liabilities, exemptions and reliefs

- Name and address of mortgagee — G14 £ 17,052

  HALIFAX PLC, BATH BRANCH ON 16 JAMES COURT, BATH

- Other liabilities

  Total of other liabilities G15 £

Net total of assets less liabilities *(box G13 less boxes G14 and G15)* G16 £147,948

- Exemptions and reliefs

  Total exemptions and reliefs G17 £

Chargeable value of assets in the UK where tax may be paid by instalments *(box G16 less box G17)* G18 £147,948

5

(Continued on next page)

Completed example of Form IHT200
Full account for personal applicants (continued)

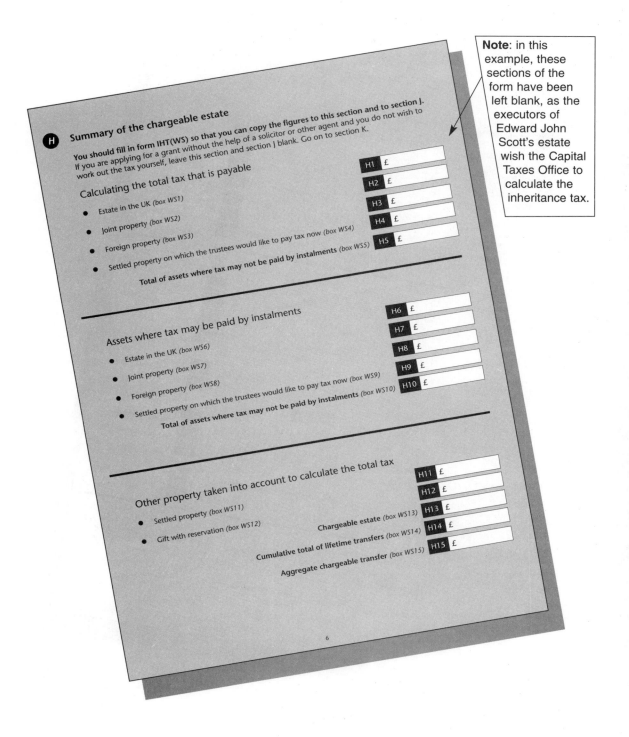

H **Summary of the chargeable estate**

You should fill in form IHT(WS) so that you can copy the figures to this section and to section J. If you are applying for a grant without the help of a solicitor or other agent and you do not wish to work out the tax yourself, leave this section and section J blank. Go on to section K.

Calculating the total tax that is payable

- Estate in the UK *(box WS1)* — H1 £
- Joint property *(box WS2)* — H2 £
- Foreign property *(box WS3)* — H3 £
- Settled property on which the trustees would like to pay tax now *(box WS4)* — H4 £

Total of assets where tax may not be paid by instalments *(box WS5)* — H5 £

Assets where tax may be paid by instalments

- Estate in the UK *(box WS6)* — H6 £
- Joint property *(box WS7)* — H7 £
- Foreign property *(box WS8)* — H8 £
- Settled property on which the trustees would like to pay tax now *(box WS9)* — H9 £

Total of assets where tax may not be paid by instalments *(box WS10)* — H10 £

Other property taken into account to calculate the total tax

- Settled property *(box WS11)* — H11 £
- Gift with reservation *(box WS12)* — H12 £

Chargeable estate *(box WS13)* — H13 £

Cumulative total of lifetime transfers *(box WS14)* — H14 £

Aggregate chargeable transfer *(box WS15)* — H15 £

6

Note: in this example, these sections of the form have been left blank, as the executors of Edward John Scott's estate wish the Capital Taxes Office to calculate the inheritance tax.

(Continued on next page)

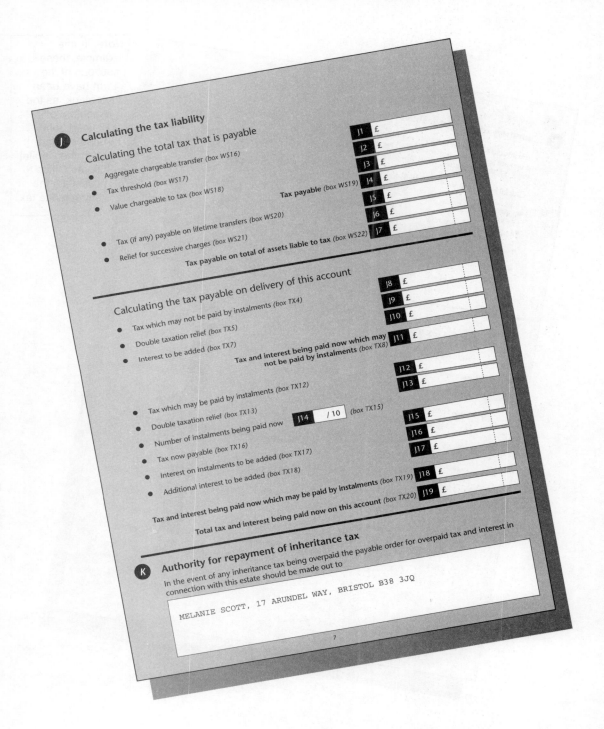

J Calculating the tax liability

Calculating the total tax that is payable

- Aggregate chargeable transfer *(box WS16)* — J1 £
- Tax threshold *(box WS17)* — J2 £
- Value chargeable to tax *(box WS18)* — J3 £
- **Tax payable** *(box WS19)* — J4 £
- — J5 £
- Tax (if any) payable on lifetime transfers *(box WS20)* — J6 £
- Relief for successive charges *(box WS21)* — J7 £

Tax payable on total of assets liable to tax *(box WS22)*

Calculating the tax payable on delivery of this account

- Tax which may not be paid by instalments *(box TX4)* — J8 £
- Double taxation relief *(box TX5)* — J9 £
- Interest to be added *(box TX7)* — J10 £

Tax and interest being paid now which may not be paid by instalments *(box TX8)* — J11 £

- Tax which may be paid by instalments *(box TX12)* — J12 £
- Double taxation relief *(box TX13)* — J13 £
- Number of instalments being paid now — J14 __ / 10 __ *(box TX15)*
- Tax now payable *(box TX16)* — J15 £
- Interest on instalments to be added *(box TX17)* — J16 £
- Additional interest to be added *(box TX18)* — J17 £

Tax and interest being paid now which may be paid by instalments *(box TX19)* — J18 £

Total tax and interest being paid now on this account *(box TX20)* — J19 £

K Authority for repayment of inheritance tax

In the event of any inheritance tax being overpaid the payable order for overpaid tax and interest in connection with this estate should be made out to

> MELANIE SCOTT, 17 ARUNDEL WAY, BRISTOL B38 3JQ

7

(Continued on next page)

Completed example of Form IHT200
Full account for personal applicants (continued)

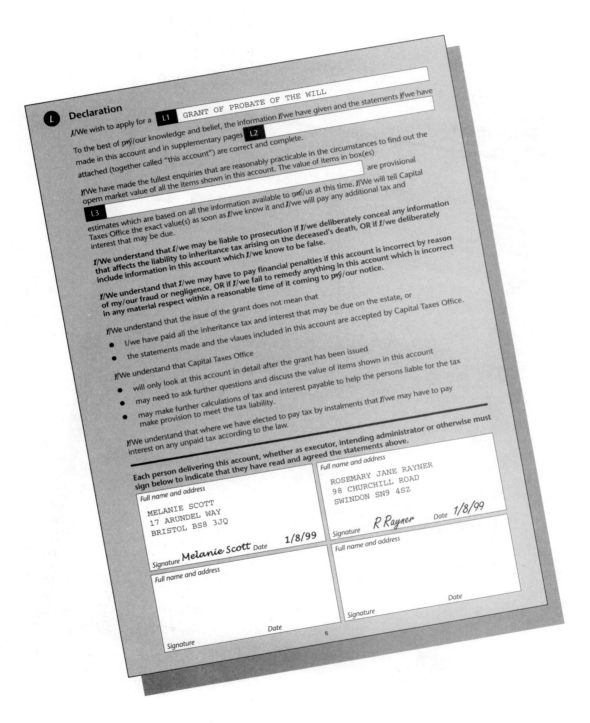

L Declaration

I/We wish to apply for a **L1** GRANT OF PROBATE OF THE WILL

To the best of my/our knowledge and belief, the information I/we have given and the statements I/we have made in this account and in supplementary pages **L2** attached (together called "this account") are correct and complete.

I/We have made the fullest enquiries that are reasonably practicable in the circumstances to find out the open market value of all the items shown in this account. The value of items in box(es) are provisional estimates which are based on all the information available to me/us at this time. I/We will tell Capital Taxes Office the exact value(s) as soon as I/we know it and I/we will pay any additional tax and interest that may be due. **L3**

I/We understand that I/we may be liable to prosecution if I/we deliberately conceal any information that affects the liability to inheritance tax arising on the deceased's death, OR if I/we deliberately include information in this account which I/we know to be false.

I/We understand that I/we may have to pay financial penalties if this account is incorrect by reason of my/our fraud or negligence, OR if I/we fail to remedy anything in this account which is incorrect in any material respect within a reasonable time of it coming to my/our notice.

I/We understand that the issue of the grant does not mean that
- I/we have paid all the inheritance tax and interest that may be due on the estate, or
- the statements made and the vlaues included in this account are accepted by Capital Taxes Office.

I/We understand that Capital Taxes Office
- will only look at this account in detail after the grant has been issued
- may need to ask further questions and discuss the value of items shown in this account
- may make further calculations of tax and interest payable to help the persons liable for the tax make provision to meet the tax liability.

I/We understand that where we have elected to pay tax by instalments that I/we may have to pay interest on any unpaid tax according to the law.

Each person delivering this account, whether as executor, intending administrator or otherwise must sign below to indicate that they have read and agreed the statements above.

Full name and address	Full name and address
MELANIE SCOTT 17 ARUNDEL WAY BRISTOL BS8 3JQ	ROSEMARY JANE RAYNER 98 CHURCHILL ROAD SWINDON SN9 4SZ
Signature *Melanie Scott* Date 1/8/99	Signature *R Rayner* Date 1/8/99
Full name and address	Full name and address
Signature Date	Signature Date

8

71

Completed example of Supplementary page D1 – The Will

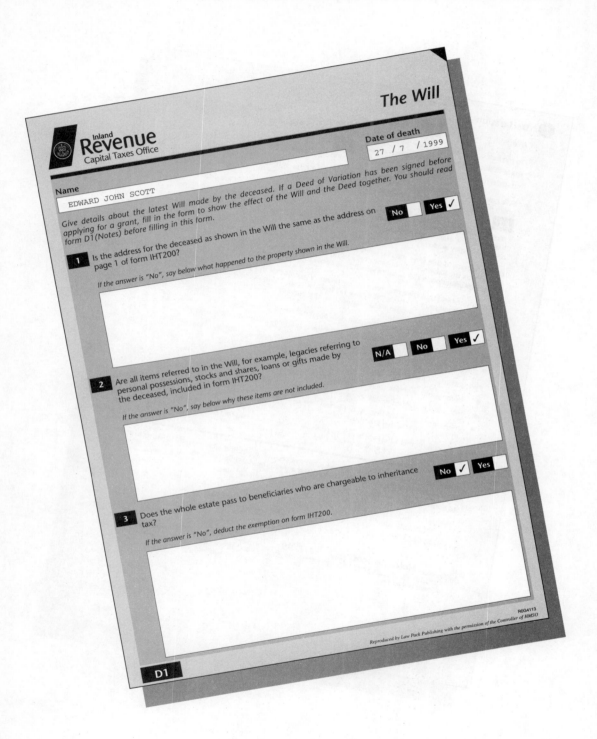

The Will

Inland Revenue
Revenue
Capital Taxes Office

Date of death 27 / 7 / 1999

Name
EDWARD JOHN SCOTT

Give details about the latest Will made by the deceased. If a Deed of Variation has been signed before applying for a grant, fill in the form to show the effect of the Will and the Deed together. You should read form D1(Notes) before filling in this form.

No ☐ Yes ✓

1 Is the address for the deceased as shown in the Will the same as the address on page 1 of form IHT200?

If the answer is "No", say below what happened to the property shown in the Will.

2 Are all items referred to in the Will, for example, legacies referring to personal possessions, stocks and shares, loans or gifts made by the deceased, included in form IHT200?

N/A ☐ No ☐ Yes ✓

If the answer is "No", say below why these items are not included.

3 Does the whole estate pass to beneficiaries who are chargeable to inheritance tax?

No ✓ Yes ☐

If the answer is "No", deduct the exemption on form IHT200.

R0G4113

D1

Completed example of Supplementary page D17
– Continuation sheet for additional information

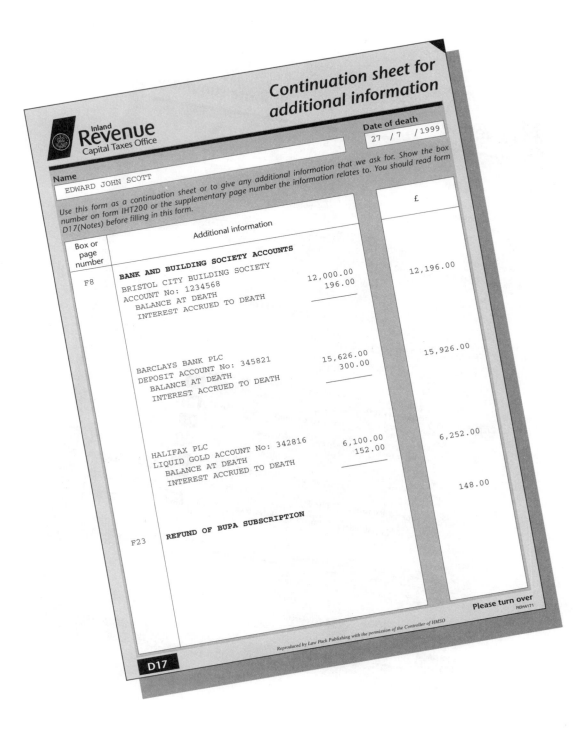

Continuation sheet for additional information

Inland **Revenue**
Capital Taxes Office

Date of death
27 / 7 / 1999

Name
EDWARD JOHN SCOTT

Use this form as a continuation sheet or to give any additional information that we ask for. Show the box number on form IHT200 or the supplementary page number the information relates to. You should read form D17(Notes) before filling in this form.

Box or page number	Additional information		£
	BANK AND BUILDING SOCIETY ACCOUNTS		
F8	BRISTOL CITY BUILDING SOCIETY		12,196.00
	ACCOUNT No: 1234568		
	BALANCE AT DEATH	12,000.00	
	INTEREST ACCRUED TO DEATH	196.00	
	BARCLAYS BANK PLC		15,926.00
	DEPOSIT ACCOUNT No: 345821		
	BALANCE AT DEATH	15,626.00	
	INTEREST ACCRUED TO DEATH	300.00	
	HALIFAX PLC		6,252.00
	LIQUID GOLD ACCOUNT No: 342816		
	BALANCE AT DEATH	6,100.00	
	INTEREST ACCRUED TO DEATH	152.00	
			148.00
F23	**REFUND OF BUPA SUBSCRIPTION**		

Please turn over
ROH4171

Reproduced by Law Pack Publishing with the permission of the Controller of HMSO

D17

Completed example of D18 Probate summary

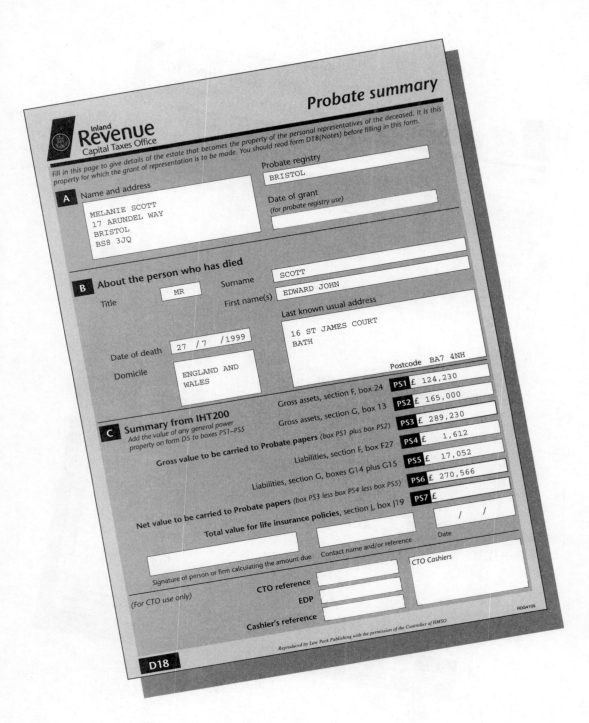

Probate summary

Inland Revenue — Capital Taxes Office

Fill in this page to give details of the estate that becomes the property of the personal representatives of the deceased. It is this property for which the grant of representation is to be made. You should read form D18(Notes) before filling in this form.

A Name and address

MELANIE SCOTT
17 ARUNDEL WAY
BRISTOL
BS8 3JQ

Probate registry

BRISTOL

Date of grant
(for probate registry use)

B About the person who has died

Title MR

Surname SCOTT

First name(s) EDWARD JOHN

Last known usual address

16 ST JAMES COURT
BATH

Postcode BA7 4NH

Date of death 27 / 7 / 1999

Domicile ENGLAND AND WALES

C Summary from IHT200
Add the value of any general power
property on form D5 to boxes PS1–PS5

Gross assets, section F, box 24	**PS1**	£ 124,230
Gross assets, section G, box 13	**PS2**	£ 165,000
Gross value to be carried to Probate papers (box PS1 plus box PS2)	**PS3**	£ 289,230
Liabilities, section F, box F27	**PS4**	£ 1,612
Liabilities, section G, boxes G14 plus G15	**PS5**	£ 17,052
Net value to be carried to Probate papers (box PS3 less box PS4 less box PS5)	**PS6**	£ 270,566
Total value for life insurance policies, section J, box J19	**PS7**	£

Signature of person or firm calculating the amount due

Contact name and/or reference

Date / /

(For CTO use only)

CTO reference

EDP

Cashier's reference

CTO Cashiers

RDG4109

Reproduced by Law Pack Publishing with the permission of the Controller of HMSO

D18

Completed example of Supplementary page D3
– Gifts and other transfers of value

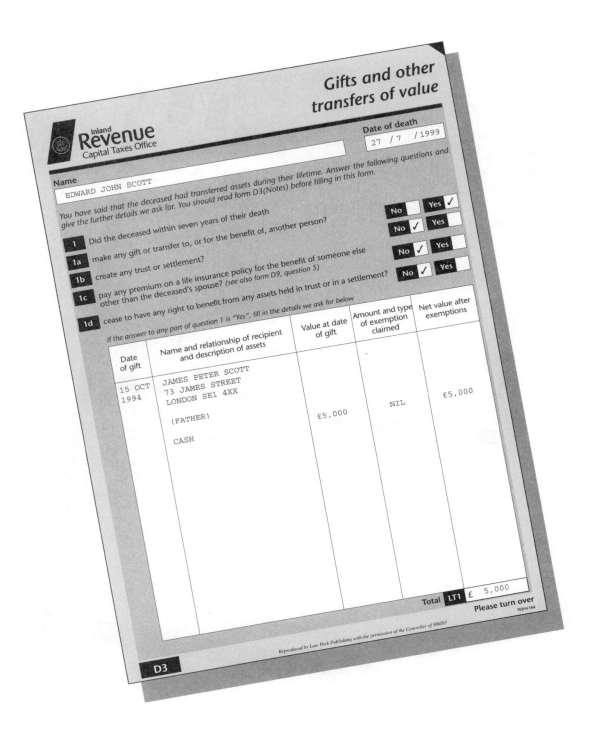

Gifts and other transfers of value

Inland Revenue Capital Taxes Office

Date of death 27 / 7 / 1999

Name EDWARD JOHN SCOTT

You have said that the deceased had transferred assets during their lifetime. Answer the following questions and give the further details we ask for. You should read form D3(Notes) before filling in this form.

1 Did the deceased within seven years of their death   No ☐   Yes ✓

1a make any gift or transfer to, or for the benefit of, another person?   No ✓   Yes ☐

1b create any trust or settlement?   No ✓   Yes ☐

1c pay any premium on a life insurance policy for the benefit of someone else other than the deceased's spouse? *(see also form D9, question 5)*   No ✓   Yes ☐

1d cease to have any right to benefit from any assets held in trust or in a settlement?   No ✓   Yes ☐

If the answer to any part of question 1 is "Yes", fill in the details we ask for below

Date of gift	Name and relationship of recipient and description of assets	Value at date of gift	Amount and type of exemption claimed	Net value after exemptions
15 OCT 1994	JAMES PETER SCOTT 73 JAMES STREET LONDON SE1 4XX (FATHER) CASH	£5,000	NIL	£5,000
			Total **LT1** £	5,000

Please turn over

RQ44164

D3

Reproduced by Law Pack Publishing with the permission of the Controller of HMSO

(Continued on next page)

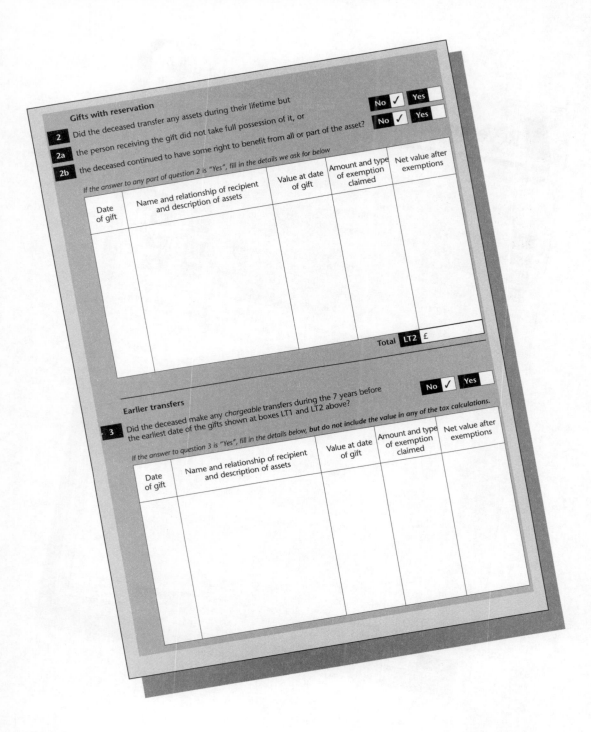

Gifts with reservation

| | | No ✓ | Yes |

2 Did the deceased transfer any assets during their lifetime but

| | | No ✓ | Yes |

2a the person receiving the gift did not take full possession of it, or

2b the deceased continued to have some right to benefit from all or part of the asset?

If the answer to any part of question 2 is "Yes", fill in the details we ask for below

Date of gift	Name and relationship of recipient and description of assets	Value at date of gift	Amount and type of exemption claimed	Net value after exemptions

Total **LT2** £

Earlier transfers

| | | No ✓ | Yes |

3 Did the deceased make any *chargeable* transfers during the 7 years before the earliest date of the gifts shown at boxes LT1 and LT2 above?

If the answer to question 3 is "Yes", fill in the details below, but do not include the value in any of the tax calculations.

Date of gift	Name and relationship of recipient and description of assets	Value at date of gift	Amount and type of exemption claimed	Net value after exemptions

Completed example of Supplementary page D4
– Joint and nominated assets

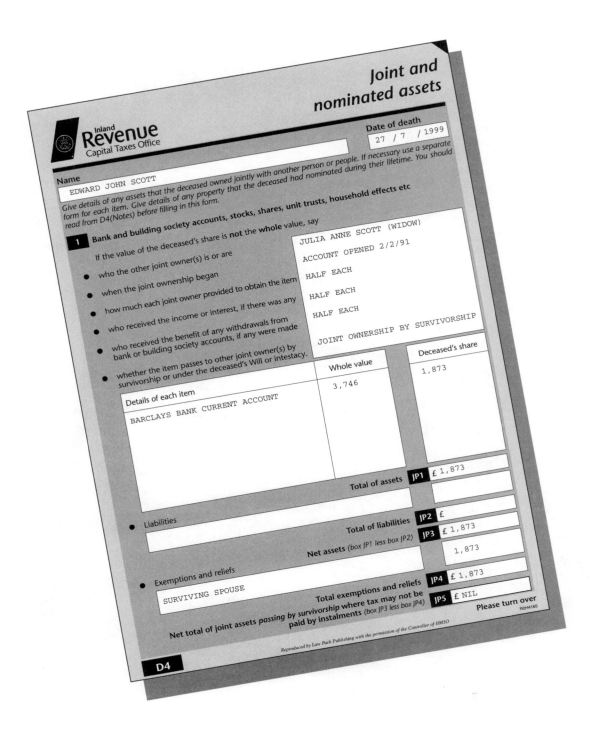

Joint and nominated assets

Inland **Revenue**
Capital Taxes Office

Date of death 27 / 7 / 1999

Name EDWARD JOHN SCOTT

Give details of any assets that the deceased owned jointly with another person or people. If necessary use a separate form for each item. Give details of any property that the deceased had nominated during their lifetime. You should read from D4(Notes) before filling in this form.

1 Bank and building society accounts, stocks, shares, unit trusts, household effects etc

If the value of the deceased's share is **not** the whole value, say

- who the other joint owner(s) is or are
- when the joint ownership began
- how much each joint owner provided to obtain the item
- who received the income or interest, if there was any
- who received the benefit of any withdrawals from bank or building society accounts, if any were made
- whether the item passes to other joint owner(s) by survivorship or under the deceased's Will or intestacy.

JULIA ANNE SCOTT (WIDOW)

ACCOUNT OPENED 2/2/91

HALF EACH

HALF EACH

HALF EACH

JOINT OWNERSHIP BY SURVIVORSHIP

Details of each item	Whole value	Deceased's share
BARCLAYS BANK CURRENT ACCOUNT	3,746	1,873

Total of assets	**JP1**	£ 1,873

- Liabilities

Total of liabilities	**JP2**	£
Net assets (box JP1 less box JP2)	**JP3**	£ 1,873
		1,873

- Exemptions and reliefs

SURVIVING SPOUSE

Total exemptions and reliefs	**JP4**	£ 1,873
Net total of joint assets *passing by survivorship where tax may not be paid by instalments* (box JP3 less box JP4)	**JP5**	£ NIL

Please turn over

R0H4165

Reproduced by Law Pack Publishing with the permission of the Controller of HMSO

D4

(Continued on next page)

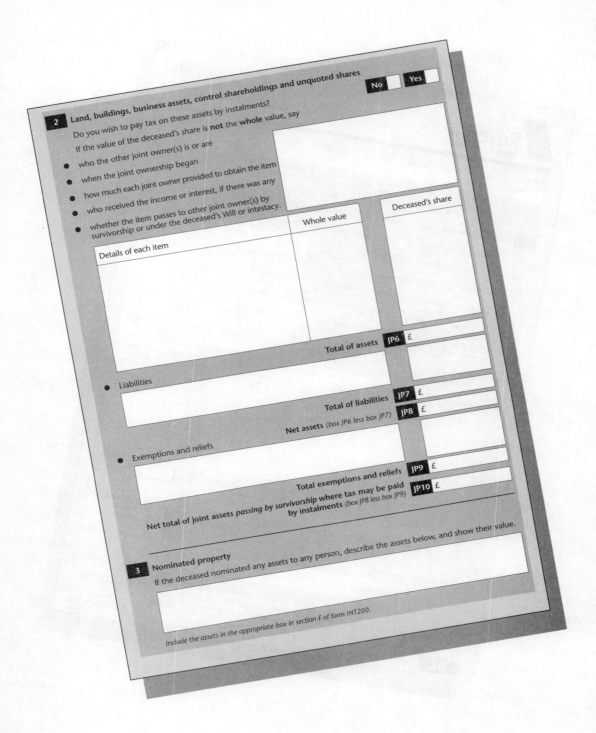

2 **Land, buildings, business assets, control shareholdings and unquoted shares**

Do you wish to pay tax on these assets by instalments? No ☐ Yes ☐

If the value of the deceased's share is **not** the **whole** value, say

- who the other joint owner(s) is or are
- when the joint ownership began
- how much each joint owner provided to obtain the item
- who received the income or interest, if there was any
- whether the item passes to other joint owner(s) by survivorship or under the deceased's Will or intestacy.

Details of each item	Whole value	Deceased's share

Total of assets	JP6	£

- Liabilities

Total of liabilities	JP7	£
Net assets *(box JP6 less box JP7)*	JP8	£

- Exemptions and reliefs

Total exemptions and reliefs	JP9	£
Net total of joint assets *passing by survivorship where tax may be paid by instalments (box JP8 less box JP9)*	JP10	£

3 **Nominated property**

If the deceased nominated any assets to any person, describe the assets below, and show their value.

Include the assets in the appropriate box in section F of form IHT200.

Completed example of Supplementary page D7 – Stocks and shares

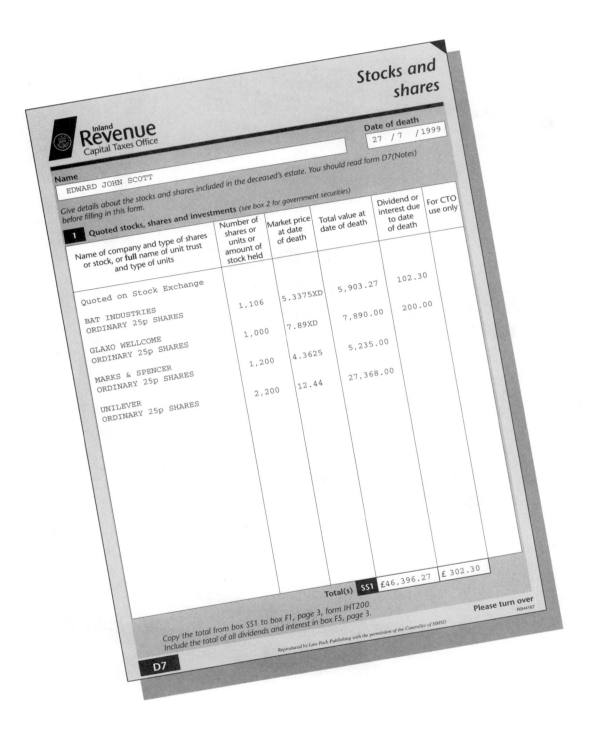

Stocks and shares

Inland Revenue — Capital Taxes Office

Date of death 27 / 7 / 1999

Name EDWARD JOHN SCOTT

Give details about the stocks and shares included in the deceased's estate. You should read form D7(Notes) before filling in this form.

1 Quoted stocks, shares and investments (see box 2 for government securities)

Name of company and type of shares or stock, or **full name of unit trust** and type of units	Number of shares or units or amount of stock held	Market price at date of death	Total value at date of death	Dividend or interest due to date of death	For CTO use only
Quoted on Stock Exchange					
BAT INDUSTRIES ORDINARY 25p SHARES	1,106	5.3375XD	5,903.27	102.30	
GLAXO WELLCOME ORDINARY 25p SHARES	1,000	7.89XD	7,890.00	200.00	
MARKS & SPENCER ORDINARY 25p SHARES	1,200	4.3625	5,235.00		
UNILEVER ORDINARY 25p SHARES	2,200	12.44	27,368.00		
Total(s) SS1			£46,396.27	£ 302.30	

Copy the total from box SS1 to box F1, page 3, form IHT200.
Include the total of all dividends and interest in box F5, page 3.

Please turn over
R0H4167

Reproduced by Law Pack Publishing with the permission of the Controller of HMSO

D7

(Continued on next page)

Completed example of Supplementary page D7
– Stocks and shares (continued)

UK Government and municipal securities

2 Description of stock	Amount of stock £	Market price at date of death	Total value at date of death	Interest due to date of death	For CTO use only
TREASURY 8% STOCK 2003	2,500	100.00	2,500.00	71.78	
Total(s) **SS2**			£ 2,500.00	£ 71.78	

Copy the total from box SS2 to box F2, page 3, form IHT200.
Include the total of all dividends and interest in box F5, page 3.

Unquoted stocks, shares and investments

3 Name of company and type of share or stock	Number of shares	Price per share	Total value of shares	Dividend due to date of death	For CTO use only
XYZ ELECTRONICS LIMITED (Registered number 1234567) Ordinary shares	2,500	1.50	3,750.00		

Include the value of the shares in box F3, page 3 or box G11, page 5, form IHT200.
Include the total of all dividends in box F5, page 3.

Traded unquoted stocks and shares

4 Name of company and type of share or stock	Number of shares	Price per share	Total value of shares	Dividend due to date of death	For CTO use only

Include the value of the shares in box F4, page 3 or box G12, page 5, form IHT200.
Include the total of all dividends in box F5, page 3.

Completed example of Supplementary page D9
– Life insurance and annuities

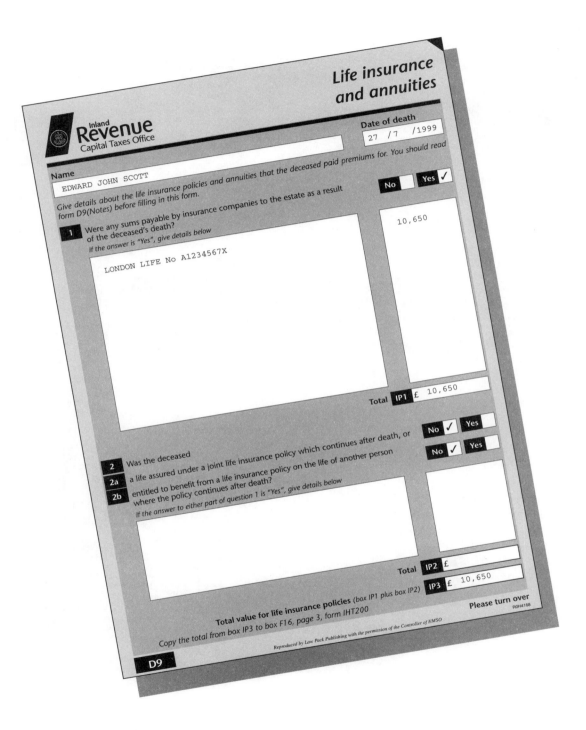

Life insurance and annuities

Inland **Revenue**
Capital Taxes Office

Date of death
27 / 7 / 1999

Name
EDWARD JOHN SCOTT

Give details about the life insurance policies and annuities that the deceased paid premiums for. You should read form D9(Notes) before filling in this form.

No ☐ Yes ✓

1 Were any sums payable by insurance companies to the estate as a result of the deceased's death?

If the answer is "Yes", give details below

LONDON LIFE No A1234567X

10,650

Total **IP1** £ 10,650

2 Was the deceased

No ✓ Yes ☐

2a a life assured under a joint life insurance policy which continues after death, or

No ✓ Yes ☐

2b entitled to benefit from a life insurance policy on the life of another person where the policy continues after death?

If the answer to either part of question 1 is "Yes", give details below

Total **IP2** £

IP3 £ 10,650

Total value for life insurance policies *(box IP1 plus box IP2)*

Copy the total from box IP3 to box F16, page 3, form IHT200

Please turn over

R0H4168

Reproduced by Law Pack Publishing with the permission of the Controller of HMSO

D9

(Continued on next page)

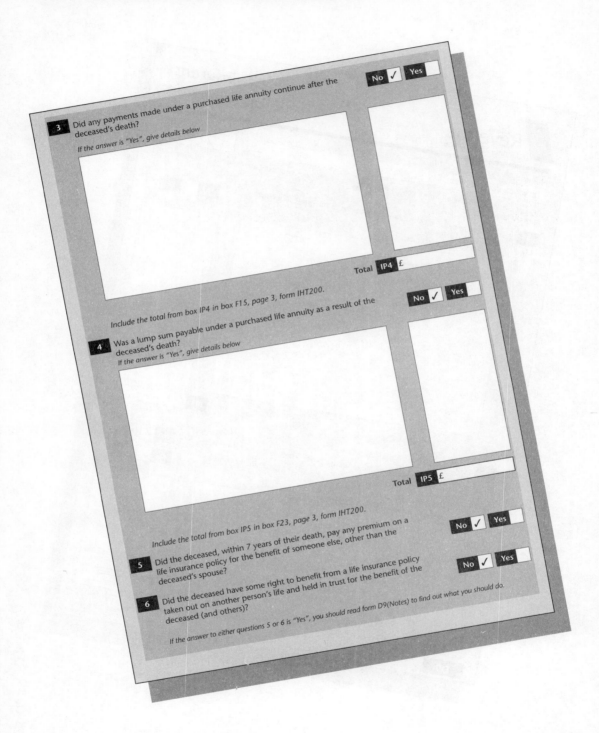

3 Did any payments made under a purchased life annuity continue after the deceased's death?

No ✓ Yes

If the answer is "Yes", give details below

Total **IP4** £

Include the total from box IP4 in box F15, page 3, form IHT200.

4 Was a lump sum payable under a purchased life annuity as a result of the deceased's death?

No ✓ Yes

If the answer is "Yes", give details below

Total **IP5** £

Include the total from box IP5 in box F23, page 3, form IHT200.

5 Did the deceased, within 7 years of their death, pay any premium on a life insurance policy for the benefit of someone else, other than the deceased's spouse?

No ✓ Yes

6 Did the deceased have some right to benefit from a life insurance policy taken out on another person's life and held in trust for the benefit of the deceased (and others)?

No ✓ Yes

If the answer to either questions 5 or 6 is "Yes", you should read form D9(Notes) to find out what you should do.

Completed example of Supplementary page D10 – Household and personal goods

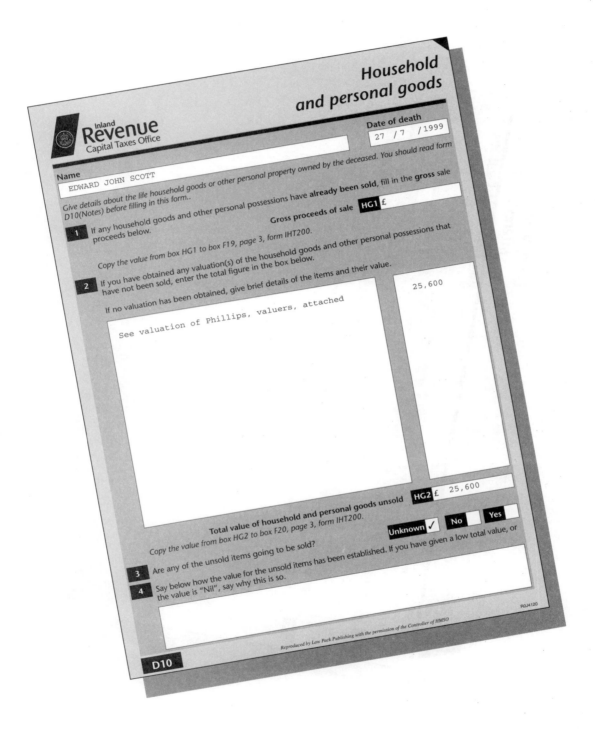

Household and personal goods

Inland Revenue Capital Taxes Office

Date of death 27 / 7 / 1999

Name EDWARD JOHN SCOTT

Give details about the life household goods or other personal property owned by the deceased. You should read form D10(Notes) before filling in this form..

1 If any household goods and other personal possessions have **already been sold**, fill in the **gross sale** proceeds below.

Gross proceeds of sale **HG1** £

Copy the value from box HG1 to box F19, page 3, form IHT200.

2 If you have obtained any valuation(s) of the household goods and other personal possessions that have not been sold, enter the total figure in the box below.

If no valuation has been obtained, give brief details of the items and their value.

25,600

See valuation of Phillips, valuers, attached

Total value of household and personal goods unsold **HG2** £ 25,600

Copy the value from box HG2 to box F20, page 3, form IHT200.

3 Are any of the unsold items going to be sold?   Unknown ✓   No   Yes

4 Say below how the value for the unsold items has been established. If you have given a low total value, or the value is "Nil", say why this is so.

D10

R0J4120

Reproduced by Law Pack Publishing with the permission of the Controller of HMSO

83

Completed example of Supplementary page D12
– Land, buildings and interests in land

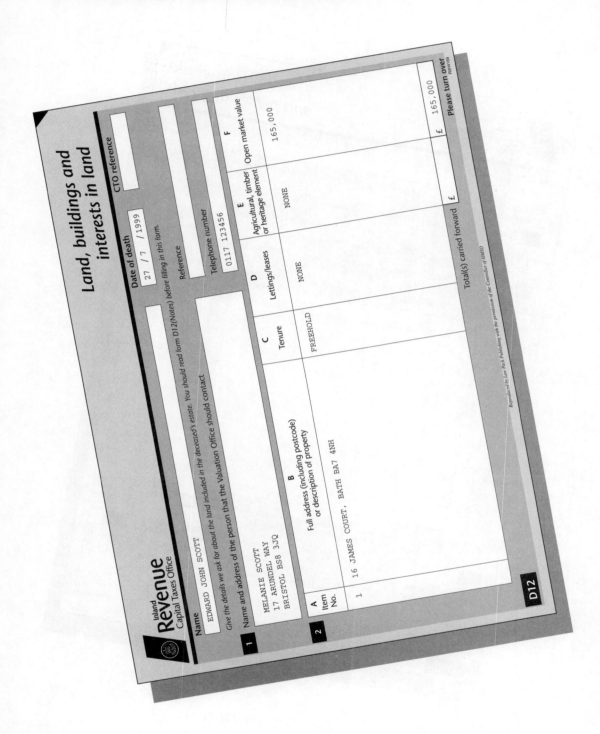

Inland Revenue Capital Taxes Office

Land, buildings and interests in land

CTO reference

Name
EDWARD JOHN SCOTT

Date of death
27 / 7 /1999

Give the details we ask for about the land included in the deceased's estate. You should read form D12(Notes) before filling in this form.

1 Name and address of the person that the Valuation Office should contact

Reference

MELANIE SCOTT
17 ARUNDEL WAY
BRISTOL BS8 3JQ

Telephone number
0117 123456

2

A Item No.	B Full address (including postcode) or description of property	C Tenure	D Lettings/leases	E Agricultural, timber or heritage element	F Open market value
1	16 JAMES COURT, BATH BA7 4NH	FREEHOLD	NONE	NONE	165,000
				Total(s) carried forward £	£ 165,000

Please turn over

Reproduced by Law Pack Publishing with the permission of the Controller of HMSO

D12

Completed example of Supplementary page D12
– Land, buildings and interests in land

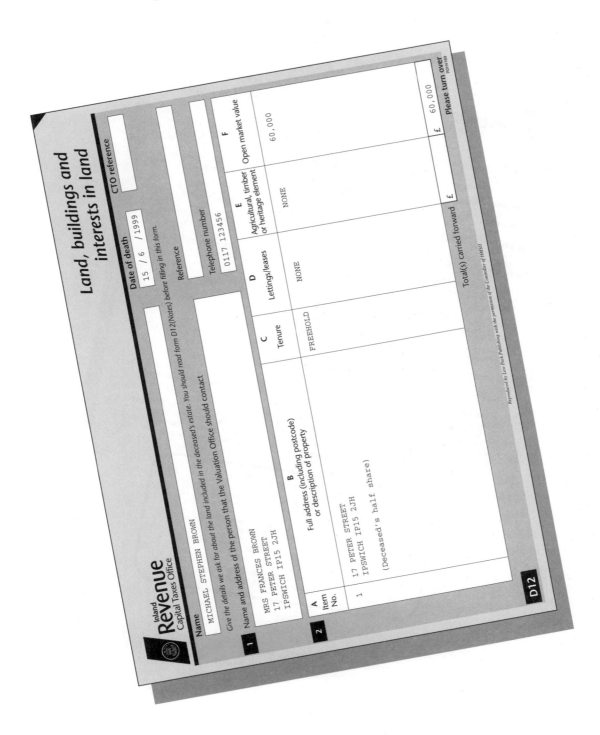

Inland Revenue
Capital Taxes Office

Land, buildings and interests in land

Name

MICHAEL STEPHEN BROWN

Give the details we ask for about the land included in the deceased's estate. You should read form D12(Notes) before filling in this form.

CTO reference

Date of death

15 / 6 / 1999

Reference

Telephone number

0117 123456

1 Name and address of the person that the Valuation Office should contact

MRS FRANCES BROWN
17 PETER STREET
IPSWICH IP15 2JH

2

A Item No.	B Full address (including postcode) or description of property	C Tenure	D Lettings/leases	E Agricultural, timber or heritage element	F Open market value
1	17 PETER STREET IPSWICH IP15 2JH (Deceased's half share)	FREEHOLD	NONE	NONE	60,000
				Total(s) carried forward	£ 60,000

£

Please turn over

RD44169

Reproduced by Law Pack Publishing with the permission of the Controller of HMSO

D12

85

Completed example of Form IHT205
– Short form for personal applicants

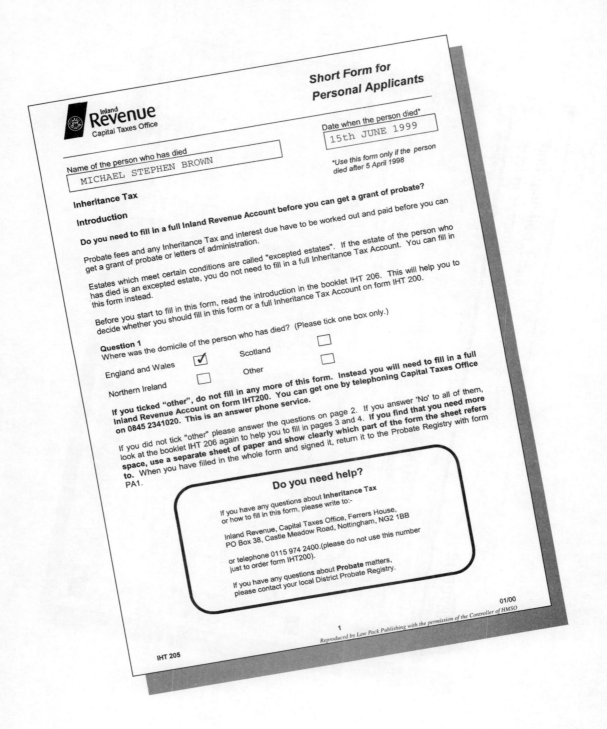

Short Form for Personal Applicants

Inland **Revenue**
Capital Taxes Office

Date when the person died*
15th JUNE 1999

Name of the person who has died

MICHAEL STEPHEN BROWN

*Use this form only if the person died after 5 April 1998

Inheritance Tax

Introduction

Do you need to fill in a full Inland Revenue Account before you can get a grant of probate?

Probate fees and any Inheritance Tax and interest due have to be worked out and paid before you can get a grant of probate or letters of administration.

Estates which meet certain conditions are called "excepted estates". If the estate of the person who has died is an excepted estate, you do not need to fill in a full Inheritance Tax Account. You can fill in this form instead.

Before you start to fill in this form, read the introduction in the booklet IHT 206. This will help you to decide whether you should fill in this form or a full Inheritance Tax Account on form IHT 200.

Question 1
Where was the domicile of the person who has died? (Please tick one box only.)

England and Wales ☑   Scotland ☐

Northern Ireland ☐   Other ☐

If you ticked "other", do not fill in any more of this form. Instead you will need to fill in a full Inland Revenue Account on form IHT200. You can get one by telephoning Capital Taxes Office on 0845 2341020. This is an answer phone service.

If you did not tick "other" please answer the questions on page 2. If you answer 'No' to all of them, look at the booklet IHT 206 again to help you to fill in pages 3 and 4. **If you find that you need more space, use a separate sheet of paper and show clearly which part of the form the sheet refers to.** When you have filled in the whole form and signed it, return it to the Probate Registry with form PA1.

Do you need help?

If you have any questions about **Inheritance Tax** or how to fill in this form, please write to:-

Inland Revenue, Capital Taxes Office, Ferrers House, PO Box 38, Castle Meadow Road, Nottingham, NG2 1BB

or telephone 0115 974 2400.(please do not use this number just to order form IHT200).

If you have any questions about **Probate** matters, please contact your local District Probate Registry.

01/00

1

Reproduced by Law Pack Publishing with the permission of the Controller of HMSO

IHT 205

(Continued on next page)

Completed example of Form IHT205
– Short form for personal applicants (continued)

Yes   No

Questions

2. Gifts

Did the person who has died within 7 years of the date they died,

a make any gifts or set up a trust? (but see note on page 2 of IHT206)   ☐ ☑

b make any payment(s) of more than £10,000 in total for the maintenance of a relative?   ☐ ☑

c pay any premiums on a life insurance policy under which the benefit is not payable to the personal representative or to the husband or wife of the person who has died?   ☐ ☑

3. Did the person who has died make a **gift with reservation** at any time?   ☐ ☑

4. Assets held in trust

Was the person who has died receiving a benefit under a trust

• at the time when they died   ☐ ☑

• at any time within 7 years before they died?   ☐ ☑

5. Foreign assets

Did the person who has died own or benefit from any assets outside the United Kingdom whose value is more than £50,000?   ☐ ☑

If you have answered 'Yes' to any of these questions, do not fill in pages 3 and 4 of this form.. Instead you will need to fill in a full Inland Revenue Account on form IHT200.

You can get one from Capital Taxes Office by telephoning our Orderline on 0845 2341020. This is an answer phone service. We will aim to send forms out to you by the end of the next working day.

2

(Continued on next page)

Return of the whole estate

Value in £s

Assets in the United Kingdom except for joint assets passing automatically to the surviving joint owner.

	Value in £s
	NIL
1. Cash other than at bank	2,592
2. Money in bank accounts	10,324
3. Money in building societies, co-operative or friendly societies or savings banks including interest to the date of death	15,500
4. Household and personal goods, for example, furniture, jewellery, car, stamp collections etc	NIL
5. Savings Certificates and other National Savings investments	NIL
6. Stocks and shares quoted on the Stock Exchange	NIL
7. Stocks and shares not quoted on the Stock Exchange	15,250
8. Insurance policies including bonuses on 'with profits' policies and mortgage protection policies ... ... See Schedule 1	53
9. Amounts which employers owe - including arrears of salary and pension payable to the estate ... State retirement pension	NIL
10. Partnership and business interests	NIL
11. Freehold and leasehold property **In the sole name of the person who has died.** (Address(es))	NIL
12. Assets held as tenants in common	
13. Any other assets not included above, for example, income tax repayment, debt or other amount owing to the person who has died ..	

Total £ [43,719] **A**

	NIL
14. Assets outside the United Kingdom (Value in sterling)	NIL
15. Nominated assets	

16. **Joint assets passing automatically to the surviving joint owner**

Details of joint assets ... ... See Schedule 2 ...

	31,321

Value of whole of joint assets £ 62,642 Value of that share
Share of person who has died (eg half) half

Total gross estate (A + 14 + 15 + 16) = £ [75,040] **B**

17. Gifts of cash, or stocks and shares quoted on the Stock Exchange ... ...

Total for excepted estate (B + 17) = £ [75,040] **C***

* see the box on the back page of this form

3

(Continued on next page)

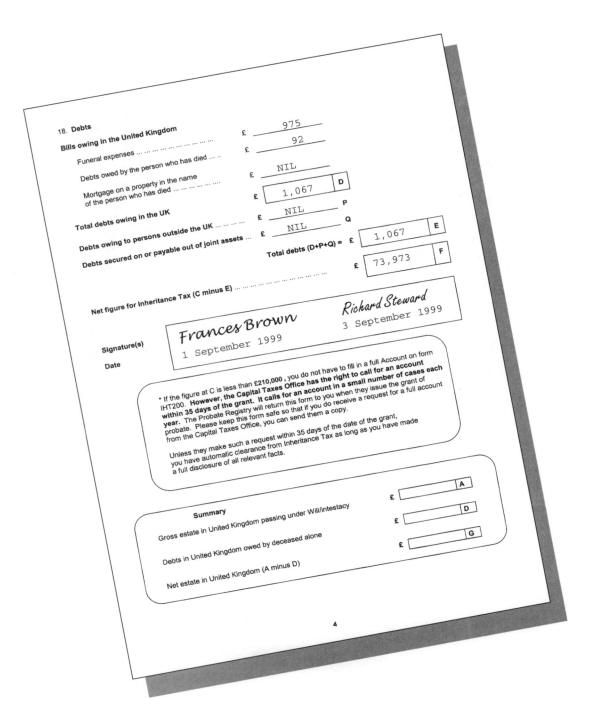

18. Debts

Bills owing in the United Kingdom

Funeral expenses ... ... £   975

Debts owed by the person who has died ... .. £   92

Mortgage on a property in the name
of the person who has died ... ... £   NIL

£   1,067   **D**

Total debts owing in the UK

Debts owing to persons outside the UK ... ... £   NIL   **P**

Debts secured on or payable out of joint assets ... £   NIL   **Q**

Total debts (D+P+Q) = £   1,067   **E**

Net figure for Inheritance Tax (C minus E) ... ... £   73,973   **F**

Signature(s)   *Frances Brown*   *Richard Steward*

Date   1 September 1999   3 September 1999

* If the figure at C is less than £210,000 , you do not have to fill in a full Account on form IHT200. **However, the Capital Taxes Office has the right to call for an account within 35 days of the grant. It calls for an account in a small number of cases each year.** The Probate Registry will return this form to you when they issue the grant of probate. Please keep this form safe so that if you do receive a request for a full account from the Capital Taxes Office, you can send them a copy.

Unless they make such a request within 35 days of the date of the grant, you have automatic clearance from Inheritance Tax as long as you have made a full disclosure of all relevant facts.

Summary

Gross estate in United Kingdom passing under Will/intestacy   £   **A**

Debts in United Kingdom owed by deceased alone   £   **D**

Net estate in United Kingdom (A minus D)   £   **G**

4

Schedules relating to completed example of Form IHT205 Short Form for Personal Applicants

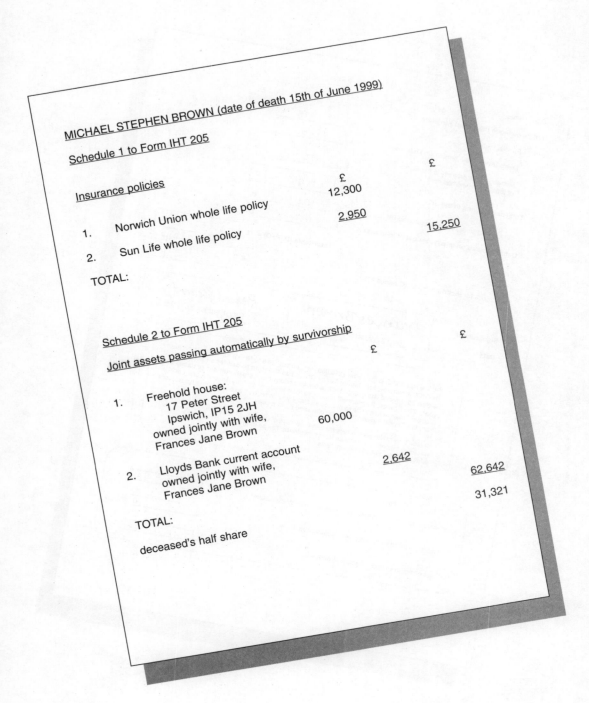

MICHAEL STEPHEN BROWN (date of death 15th of June 1999)

Schedule 1 to Form IHT 205

	£	£
Insurance policies	12,300	
1. Norwich Union whole life policy	2,950	
2. Sun Life whole life policy		15,250
TOTAL:		

Schedule 2 to Form IHT 205

Joint assets passing automatically by survivorship

	£	£
1. Freehold house: 17 Peter Street Ipswich, IP15 2JH owned jointly with wife, Frances Jane Brown	60,000	
2. Lloyds Bank current account owned jointly with wife, Frances Jane Brown	2,642	62,642
TOTAL:		31,321

deceased's half share

Completed example of Form Con 40 – Stock transfer

STOCK TRANSFER FORM

(Above this line for Registrars only)

Certificate lodged with the Registrar

(For completion by the Registrar/Stock Exchange)

Consideration Money £ NIL

Name of Undertaking	MARKS & SPENCER PLC	**Figures**
Description of Security	ORDINARY 25P SHARES	(600 units of 25P)

Number or amount of Shares, Stock or other security and, in figures column only, number and denomination of units, if any.

Words

SIX HUNDRED

In the name(s) of

EDWARD JOHN SCOTT OF 16 JAMES COURT, BATH BA7 4NH

Names(s) of registered holder(s) should be given in full: the address should be given where there is only one holder.

BY HIS PERSONAL REPRESENTATIVES, MELANIE SCOTT AND ROSEMARY JANE RAYNER

If the transfer is not made by the registered holder(s) insert also the name(s) and capacity (e.g. Executor(s)) of the person(s) making the transfer).

I/We hereby transfer the above security out of the name(s) aforesaid to the person(s) named below.

Stamp of Selling Broker(s) or, for transactions which are not stock exchange transactions, of Agent(s), if any, acting for the Transferor(s)

Signature(s) of transferor(s)

1. *Melanie Scott*

2. *R Rayner*

Date 10TH JULY 1999

3. ....

4. ....
Bodies corporate should execute under their common seal

Full name(s) and full postal address(es) (including County or, if applicable, Postal District number) of the person(s) to whom the security is transferred

MRS. ROSEMARY JANE RAYNER
98 CHURCHILL ROAD
SWINDON SN9 4SZ

Please state title, if any, or whether Mr., Mrs. or Miss.

Please complete in typewriting or Block Capitals

I/We request that such entries be made in the register as are necessary to give effect to this transfer.

Stamp or name and address of person lodging this form (if other than the buying broker(s))

Stamp of Buying Broker(s) (if any)

MELANIE SCOTT
17 ARUNDEL WAY
BRISTOL BS8 3JQ

Reproduced by Law Pack Publishing with the permission of the Controller of HMSO

(Continued on next page)

FORM OF CERTIFICATE REQUIRED FOR EXEMPTION FROM STAMP DUTY

Instruments of transfer executed on or after 1 May 1987 are exempt from stamp duty when the transaction falls within one of the following categories and will not need to be seen in stamp offices provided they are certified as below in accordance with the Stamp Duty (Exempt Instruments) Regulations 1987.

A. The vesting of property subject to a trust in the trustees of the trust on the appointment of a new trustee, or in the continuing trustees on the retirement of a trustee.

B. The conveyance or transfer of property which forms part of an intestate's estate to the person entitled on intestacy (or his nominee).

C. The conveyance or transfer of property within section 84(4) of the Finance Act 1985 (death: appropriation in satisfaction of a general legacy of money) or section 84(5) or (7) of that Act (death: appropriation in satisfaction of any interest of surviving spouse and in Scotland also of any interest of issue).

D. The appropriation of property within section 84(4) of the Finance Act 1985 (death: appropriation in satisfaction of a general legacy of money) or section 84(5) or (7) of that Act (death: appropriation in satisfaction of any interest of surviving spouse and in Scotland also of any interest of issue).

E. The conveyance or transfer of property which forms part of the residuary estate of a testator to a beneficiary (or his nominee) entitled solely by virtue of his entitlement under the will.

F. The conveyance or transfer of property out of a settlement in or towards satisfaction of a beneficiary's interest, not being an interest acquired for money or money's worth, being a conveyance or transfer constituting a distribution of property in accordance with the provisions of the settlement.

G. The conveyance or transfer of property on and in consideration only of marriage to a party to the marriage (or his nominee) or to trustees to be held on terms of a settlement made in consideration only of the marriage.

H. The conveyance or transfer of property within section 83(1) of the Finance Act 1985 (transfers in connection with divorce etc.)

I. The conveyance or transfer of property by the liquidator of property which formed part of the assets of the company in liquidation to a shareholder of that company (or his nominee) in or towards satisfaction of the shareholder's rights on a winding up.

J. The grant in fee simple of an easement in or over land for no consideration in money or money's worth.

K. The grant of a servitude for no consideration in money or money's worth.

L. The conveyance or transfer of property operating as a voluntary disposition inter vivos for no consideration in money or money's worth nor any consideration referred to in section 57 of the Stamp Act 1891 (conveyance in consideration of a debt etc.)

M. The conveyance or transfer of property by an instrument within section 84(1) of the Finance Act 1985 (death: varying disposition).

I/We certify that this instrument falls within category (1) ..E.. in the Schedule to the Stamp Duty (Exempt Instruments) Regulations 1987 set out above.

I/We, not being the transferor, grantor, or the solicitor(s) thereof, hereby state that I/we are authorised to sign this certificate and that I/we give the certificate from my/our knowledge of the facts stated in it.

(1) Insert A or B or appropriate category.

(2) Delete this paragraph if not applicable.

(3) To be signed by transferor or grantor or by solicitor or duly authorised agent.

(4) Where signed by person not transferor, grantor or solicitor, state capacity in which signed.

Dated the ..10TH.. day of ..JULY.. 19 ..99..

(4) Description or capacity of signatory

EXECUTOR

(3) Signatory

Melanie Scott   EXECUTOR

R Rayner

FORM OF CERTIFICATE REQUIRED WHERE TRANSFER IS NOT LIABLE TO AD VALOREM STAMP DUTY
(50 Pence fixed duty payable)

Some instruments of transfer are liable to a fixed duty of 50p when the transaction falls within one of the following categories - for which the certificate below may be completed.

(1) Transfer by way of security for a loan or re-transfer to the original transferor on repayment of a loan.

(2) Transfer, not on sale and not arising under any contract of sale and where no beneficial interest in the property passes: (a) to a person who is a mere nominee of, and is nominated only by, the transferor; (b) from a mere nominee who has at all times held the property on behalf of the transferor; (c) from one nominee to another nominee of the same beneficial owner where the first nominee has at all times held the property on behalf of that beneficial owner. (NOTE - This category does not include a transfer made in any of the following circumstances: (i) by a holder of stock, etc., following the grant of an option to purchase the stock, to the person entitled to the option or his nominee; (ii) to a nominee in contemplation of a contract for the sale of the stock, etc., then about to be entered into; (iii) from the nominee of a vendor, who has instructed the nominee orally or by some unstamped writing to hold stock, etc., in trust for a purchaser, to such purchaser.)

I/We hereby certify that the transaction in respect of which this transfer is made is one which falls within the category ....+ above. I/We confirm that I/we have been duly authorised by the transferor to sign this certificate and that the facts of the transaction are within my/our knowledge.

+ Insert (1) or (2):

Here set out the facts concisely explaining the transaction, in cases falling within (1) or (2) or in any other case where 50p fixed duty is offered.

Description ("Transferor", "Solicitor", etc.)

Signature(s)

Date

Completed example of Form AS1
– Assent of whole of registered title(s)

HM Land Registry **AS1**

Assent of whole of registered title(s)

(if you need more room than is provided for in a panel, use continuation sheet CS and staple to this form)

1. Title Number(s) of the Property *(leave blank if not yet registered)*

XYZ 123456

2. Property

16 JAMES COURT, BATH BA7 4NH

If this assent is made under section 37 of the Land Registration Act 1925 following a not-yet-registered dealing with part only of the land in a title, or is made under rule 72 of the Land Registration Rules 1925, include a reference to the last preceding document of title containing a description of the property.

3. Date

30/5/99

4. Name of deceased proprietor *(give full names)*

EDWARD JOHN SCOTT

5. Personal Representative of deceased proprietor *(give full names and Company's Registered Number if any)*

MELANIE SCOTT of 17 Arundel Way, Bristol BS8 3JQ and
ROSEMARY JANE RAYNER of 98 Churchill Road, Swindon SN9 4SZ

6. Recipient for entry on the register *(Give full names and Company's Registered Number if any: for Scottish Co. Reg. Nos. use an SC prefix. For foreign companies give territory in which incorporated.)*

MELANIE SCOTT

Unless otherwise arranged with Land Registry headquarters, a certified copy of the transferee's constitution (in English or Welsh) will be required if it is a body corporate but is not a company registered in England and Wales or Scotland under the Companies Acts.

7. Recipient's intended address(es) for service in the U.K. (including postcode) for entry on the register

17 ARUNDEL WAY, BRISTOL BS8 3JQ

8. The Personal Representative assents to the vesting of the property in the Recipient.

9. The Personal Representative assents with *(place "X" in the box which applies and add any modifications)*

☐ full title guarantee   ☑ limited title guarantee

10. Declaration of trust *Where there is more than one recipient, place "X" in the appropriate box.*

☐ The recipients are to hold the property on trust for themselves as joint tenants.

☐ The recipients are to hold the property on trust for themselves as tenants in common in equal shares.

☐ The recipients are to hold the property *(complete as necessary)*

Crown copyright (ref: LR/SC.3)

Reproduced by Law Pack Publishing with the permission of the Controller of HMSO

(Continued on next page)

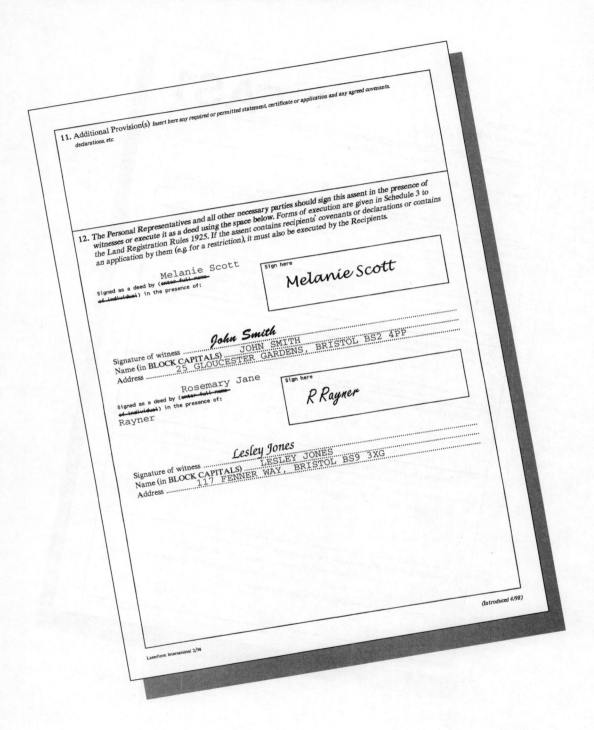

11. Additional Provision(s) *Insert here any required or permitted statement, certificate or application and any agreed covenants.* declarations, etc.

12. The Personal Representatives and all other necessary parties should sign this assent in the presence of witnesses or execute it as a deed using the space below. Forms of execution are given in Schedule 3 to the Land Registration Rules 1925. If the assent contains recipients' covenants or declarations or contains an application by them (e.g. for a restriction), it must also be executed by the Recipients.

Signed as a deed by (enter full name of individual) in the presence of:

Melanie Scott

Sign here

Melanie Scott

Signature of witness ...... *John Smith*
Name (in **BLOCK CAPITALS**) ...... JOHN SMITH
Address ...... 25 GLOUCESTER GADENS, BRISTOL BS2 4PP

Signed as a deed by (enter full name of individual) in the presence of:

Rosemary Jane Rayner

Sign here

R Rayner

Signature of witness ...... *Lesley Jones*
Name (in **BLOCK CAPITALS**) ...... LESLEY JONES
Address ...... 117 FENNER WAY, BRISTOL BS9 3XG

(Introduced 4/98)

Laserform International 2/98

Index

administrator 3

assent 42

assets of deceased 19
   checklist 20
   jointly held 15
   transfer of 41

bank account 22

beneficiaries 10, 18
   as administrators 3
   identifying 18

Bonds & Stock Office 26

capital gains tax 44

Capital Taxes Office 29

conveyance 43

Council Tax 27

creditors, unknown 18

death
   certificate 8
   registering of 7

estate 1
   insolvent 2

executors 1, 13
   multiple 2

financial records 17

final accounts 43

first applicant 2

funeral 9
   expenses 20

gifts & legacies 41

Girobank 38

grant of letters of administration
   with the will annexed 3

High Court 2

income tax 27

Inheritance (Provision for
   Family and Dependants) Act
   1975 xiii, 43

inheritance tax 17, 36
   means of paying 37–39

Inland Revenue 15, 17, 21

intestacy 3, 45–46
   succession on 45–46

Last Will & Testament 9–11

life assurance 27

life interest 4

Lloyd's of London 5

London Gazette 18

minors, as executors 3

mortgage 22

National Savings 15, 17, 26, 37

PAYE *see* income tax

pension 27, 28, 38

personal representative 3

power reserved letter 2

Premium Bonds 15, 17, 26

probate
    fees 35
    grant of 1, 14, 29
    overview xi

probate forms 16, 29
    Form AS1 – Assent of whole of
      registered title 42, 92
    Form AS3 42
    Form 920 44
    Form Con 40 42, 90
    Form NSA 904 15, 25, 26
    Form IHT200 Full Account
      for Personal Applicants
      26–27, 29, 30–34, 36, 64
    Form IHT205 Short Form for
      Personal Applicants 29–33,
      35, 86
    Form IHT206 29, 33
    Form IHT213 29, 33
    Form NSA 904 15, 25
    Form PA1 Probate application
      form 29, 30–32, 60
    Form R185 (Estate Income)
      xiii, 44

Supplementary pages
    D1 – The Will 72
    D3 – Gifts and other transfers
      of value 33, 75
    D4 – Joint and nominated
      assets 33, 77
    D5 33
    D6 33
    D7 – Stocks and shares 33, 79
    D12 – Land, buildings and
      interest in land 33, 34, 84
    D15 – Foreign property 28
    D17 – Continuation sheet
      79
    D18 – Probate summary
      30–31, 36, 74

Probate Registry 15,23,28,46

property 21
    foreign 28
    nominated 15
    registered land 42
    unregistered land 42

Registrar of Births and
    Deaths 7–8

salary payments 26

Social Fund 20

Social Security payments 28

solicitors 5

Stock Exchange Daily Official
    List 23

stocks and shares 23–24

taxation of estate 44

testator 1

transfer of property (assent) 42

works of art 25